THE
POWER
of
MERCY

BERNARD O. APPIAH

ISBN: 978-9988-2-2236-9
ISBN: 978-9988-2-2237-6

For enquiries contact the author:
Email: otopah01@yahoo.co.uk
Tel: 00 44 7572 612 947

Printed in the UK.
Lightning Source (UK) Ltd
Chapter House
Pitfield
Kiln Farm
Milton Keynes,
Buckinghamshire
MK11 3LW,
United Kingdom

Ingram Content Group
1 Ingram Blvd
La Vergne, TN 37086
United States

Lightning Source Australia PTY Ltd.
1246 Heil Quaker Blvd
Unit A1/A3 7Janine Street VIC 3179
Australia

Design: *www.print-innovation.com*

DEDICATION

To all present and future members of The Life Word Centre (TLWC).

ACKNOWLEDGEMENTS

I give all praise and thanks to my God, who in His infinite mercy has brought into manifestation a dream he showed me about twenty-five ago. I had as an author displayed books at a function. What a faithful God He is? I am forever indebted to Him.

I appreciate all the efforts and the role everyone played in my physical and spiritual well-being. All members of the Agyen-Frempong and Appiah Otopah families, whose love, sacrifices and discipline have pushed me this far in life.

I also appreciate all those who have assisted me in diverse ways in my ministry over the years. I am very grateful and pray that God's mercy would find you.

Special thanks to my sister Mrs Anita Adjei Frempong who proof-read and edited this material.

To my wife, Lady Julie and children – Chrystabel, Faith and Leon you're just great.

35 Then it happened, as He was coming near Jericho, that a certain blind man sat by the road begging. 36 And hearing a multitude passing by, he asked what it meant. 37 So they told him that Jesus of Nazareth was passing by. 38 And he cried out, saying, "Jesus, Son of David, have mercy on me!"

39 Then those who went before warned him that he should be quiet; but he cried out all the more, "Son of David, have mercy on me!"

40 So Jesus stood still and commanded him to be brought to Him. And when he had come near, He asked him, 41 saying, "What do you want Me to do for you?"

He said, "Lord, that I may receive my sight."

42 Then Jesus said to him, "Receive your sight; your faith has made you well." 43 And immediately he received his sight, and followed Him, glorifying God. And all the people, when they saw it, gave praise to God. (Luke 18:35-43)

INTRODUCTION

Different people on the basis of their circumstances today understand *mercy* differently. From the social, political, ecclesiastical, theological standpoint there may be diverse definitions and meanings of *mercy* but one thing in common in the meaning of mercy is that it can be traced to the very core of humanity in their dealings and relationships with others. From a biblical standpoint, man is a product of God and therefore the exercise of mercy originate from God. There would be no better understanding of the subject except we explore what mercy means to God and how He exercised mercy. In spite of the fact that this mercy is part of the core of every human, God decided to demonstrate mercy to us through His Son Jesus Christ who by Himself is the embodiment of God, that through Him we may understand the mercy of God in its very perfect state. It is to say that we cannot exercise mercy in our dealings with our fellow humans until we understand the depth of God's *mercy* towards us.

We turn to the scriptures to explore the subject of mercy from the Old Testament perspective of the institutionalisation of mercy in the relationship that God had with man. The Subject has also been looked at from the New Testament to indicate the implication of the scriptural understanding of God's *mercy* for us today. I have therefore used the above quoted biblical narrative as a bridge to explore the idea of *mercy* that seem to be a life-changing virtue of God in His dealing with Humankind under the old and new covenants. However, we cannot start our exploration without first examining the narrative employed as tools for this exploration.

CONTENTS

Chapter One

A CONDITION BEYOND DISABILITY

These days when people are building houses and offices, they are asked to take into consideration those who are disabled to the extent that in certain countries there are strict regulations as to what you need to put into a building to make it disability-friendly. This is to allow people in wheelchairs and with other mobility impairments to use public places more easily and more safely. But in biblical times if you had a disability like the man in the scriptural text had, it was even impossible to get a job in order to earn a living. And all you were reduced to was to sit somewhere by the roadside and beg for alms and to depend on the largesse of people.

Disability in history

Society in biblical times, have not as yet advanced to make life more convenient for the disabled. It could have also been so because disability such as this man had was considered in some instances as punishment from God to that particular individual or even in some cases the consequence of the disabled's parents' sins. As a result not much attention was paid to the disabled. We have an insight into the public perception of disability during the biblical era when in John 9, Jesus heals a young blind man then the disciples then asks Jesus if it was the mother or the father that had sinned.

The story wasn't very different from medieval times. For example in medieval England, attitudes to disability were mixed. People thought it was a punishment for sin, or the result of being born under the hostile influence of the planet Saturn. From medieval Roman Catholic perspective, they believed that disabled people were closer to God - they were suffering purgatory on earth rather than after death and would get to heaven sooner. Also there was no state provision for people with disabilities as we may have today in a lot of developed countries.

At some point in the development of the awareness of disability, most lived and worked in their communities, supported by family and friends. If they couldn't work, their town or village might support them, but sometimes people resorted to begging. They were mainly cared for by monks and nuns who sheltered pilgrims and strangers as their Christian duty.[1]

As history suggests, in 1388 The Statute of Cambridge ("Poor Law"): distinguishes between the "deserving" and "undeserving" poor claiming alms. Disabled and older people are considered to be "deserving" and therefore eligible for charity. Further to the law and the classification of disability, in the 1530s the dissolution of the monasteries created large numbers of Beggars, many of them disabled people who had previously been supported by the church. In response the Poor Law Act of 1535 decrees that "the poor and impotent" should be supported by way of voluntary and charitable alms raised locally. This was the beginning of taxation to support the poor.[2]

Meet the beggar Jesus met

From the scriptural text, the visually challenged man was seated by the road and heard that Jesus was passing by. Even though the bible does not give enough background information of the man, it could be said that the blind man had heard of what Jesus Christ of Nazareth was able to do. This made him to shout "Jesus Son of David, Have Mercy on me." Jesus with his disciples were passing by. Examining the history of disability and the challenges associated with it, there is no question whatsoever how unhappy disabled people were at the time. The visually impaired man's situation might have saddened him over the years probably for the fact that he might have had very good plans for his life and thought life would have treated him better than it has. Even in his state of disability, he might have believed in himself that if he had the opportunity to see, he could still do something significant with his life. Also he might have also convinced himself that if he had the opportunity to see again he could make up for lost time and the years of under-achievement in his life.

The bottom line was that he needed some sort of help for that break he needed in his life to set him on course for a life of significance. He couldn't help himself out of the situation he was in. It is possible that even in his daily routine of depending on the graciousness of people to earn a Living, he might have needed the help of others to bring him to the spot where he sat to beg for the alms. He found himself in a situation where he knew he couldn't help himself and therefore needed someone to get him out of his misery and predicament.

However, when the man heard of Jesus passing by, he did something quite remarkable, which made Jesus stop to listen to him. In the first instance he never asked for healing until the time Jesus stopped and asked that he be brought to him and subsequently asking him what he was requiring from Him. He asked for mercy. He cried out for mercy, which was a bit more than just asking for healing for his blindness to be able to see. And as we get into his mind through the language he used to understand his request of mercy in the proceeding chapter. It is clear in that discussion that he just didn't want to see as a form of restoration. Consider that this man had classmates, peers, friends and family members of similar age who might have gone ahead of him in life because disability during his era was some sort of a condemnation to a life of destitution and deprivation. It would not just be enough to let him see, as even that would have placed him on a back foot.

A right perspective leading to an accurate assessment

It is worth-noting that the visually challenged man seem to have a clear perspective to what his limitations were through his own personal assessment, and for that matter knew exactly the sort of help he needed to move to a place of parity if not beyond those that have gone ahead of Him. Having the right perspective to issues and certain circumstances helps in the process of interrogating situations and obtaining vital information to understand it, and subsequently seeking the right sort of help. Every individual has his or her own perspective to things, which is unique to them. Perspective or even in a much broader sense worldview is how we see things and interpret the things we see and experience. It is the lens each one of us wears through which we see the world and interpret the world around us. It has a very profound influence on almost every area of our lives, namely; health, beliefs systems, attitude, recognizing opportunity, lifestyle and work.

Perspective can positively and negatively affects us. Let take two examples as illustrations to understand what perspective or worldview is all about. First, a shoe company sent two sales executives to a town whose inhabitants didn't wear shoes. Upon arrival, Sales Executive A called the corporate HQ, that based on the market condition, he would need a lot more shoes sent over and that the initial consignment was not going to be enough. Sales Executive B, upon arrival in the town also called the corporate HQ, and said it was useless to have come to the town to sell shoes because the people didn't wear shoes and so the consignment had to be cancelled.

To analyse the actions of the two sales executives using perspective and worldview as the framework of analysis, it is evident that Sales Executive A, saw opportunity due to the fact that the inhabitants of the town didn't wear shoes however, Sales executive B saw no market for the products altogether because, the people didn't wear shoes. The two executives were confronted with the same conditions but each saw, experienced and analysed the situation differently thereby leading to the conclusions each of them made. Executive A saw the situation and analysed it from an abundant-opportunity mentality' perspective whilst Executive B saw the situation and analysed it from a 'scarcity –misfortune mentality'. Their perspective and worldview had a great bearing on how they saw what they saw and the kind of conclusions they each drew from the experience. Certainly the visually challenged man saw and analysed his meeting with Jesus from an 'abundant-opportunity mentality' and therefore asked for more than just enough to set him on par with his colleagues and peers. He saw an opportunity to become just more than the blind man that sat near Jericho who is now healed.

The second illustration is about giving a description of a drinking glass with water. A couple of years ago, I was teaching on the subject of mentality and how our perspective and worldview is greatly influenced by our mental framework of thinking - mentality. By mentality I meant the mental framework based on which all information that goes through our mind is analysed, subsequently draw conclusions and form the basis to take action or make decisions. I took a glass of water as part of my illustration and poured water into the glass about halfway the volume capacity of the glass. I subsequently lifted the glass and called a few people to describe the glass and its content. A couple of people said the glass was half empty others also said it was half full. I then explained those that were seeing the glass half-full were seeing with a positive perspective – 'abundant-opportunity mentality', which relates to a right mental framework and those that saw the glass half-empty with water were seeing from a negative perspective – 'scarcity-misfortune mentality'.

Combining these two illustrations and how that depicts the concept of perspective and worldview, it is evident that the visually impaired man in the scriptural narrative crying out to Jesus for mercy, had the right perspective and worldview which informed him of the choice of action he needed from

Jesus. He could have just asked for his blindness to be cured but instead requested for more. At some points in our lives we pray, and whether we pray for ourselves or for others, for the Lord to do something in our lives or in lives of others, we need to pray the right kind of prayers and that only comes through having the right perspective to whatever circumstances and situations you find yourself in. It is understandable that sometimes we fall short of the ability to put our feelings, pain, frustrations and stresses into words. And that is partly the reason why the Holy Spirit makes intercession for us in utterances and groans we cannot understand. And that is because He can feel what we feel because we have the privilege of having a high priest who has been through what we may be going through now and have the capability to see us through or get us out of it.

A Confident Approach

When we approach God with a 'scarcity-misfortune mentality–laden' prayer we limit him and cut Him out fully expressing who He is to us and His modus operandi. The reason for this line of thought is that His Word says ' open your mouth wide and He'll fill it' (Psalm 81:10), he also says the He is able to do exceedingly abundantly above what you can think or ask (Eph 3:20). There are some of us who also approach God as though we are a bother to Him and therefore prefer not to ask 'too much' from Him. We decide to take a modest approach in our asking of the Lord or pouring out our hearts to the Lord. And so we are unable to pour out our hearts before Him, acknowledging that He's a true father. Even if what you ask is superfluous He still understands and will still do for you what in His sovereignty and wisdom is best for you. You have to understand that God is eternal – not restricted to time, and He's not limited – all things belong to Him and therefore we can feel as free around Him as our heavenly father, in the same way as earthly children feel free around their earthly father and ask anything. I can only imagine the number of times my children will run to me from the TV room to me anywhere I may be around the house asking me to buy an item that was advertised on the kids' channel they were watching. They ask confidently knowing that they will have it. This is the beauty of the relationship we have with our Lord Jesus Christ. We can ask of Him anything confidently and be assured that so long as it is in the will of God, He will answer.

We can admire this visually challenged man for the confidence he had in Jesus not just to ask that his disability be dealt with and maybe try to find some means later to deal with the other things that bothered him or to seek solutions from elsewhere to take care of the other things that could equally be a challenge after he was able to see. His attitude was like, if he can heal me of my blindness, then He can and might as well deal with its associated issues too. The visually challenged man therefore cried for mercy instead of asking that his blindness be healed.

Chapter Two

THE CALL OUT OF SINCERITY

Besides the issues of perspective and world-view and his confident approach to seeking the attention of Jesus, the other thing that made Jesus stop and speak to the man and ask him "What exactly do you want me to do for you?" although he had been crying out loud attempting to be louder than the crowd's noise was because of his sincerity. The man was not a 'Christian', an ardent follower of Jesus Christ. He was a Jew and during Jesus' time Jesus and his movement were considered by some sections of society as a false religion, others considered them a sect of Judaism. As a matter of fact the word 'Christian' at the time was a derogatory term to mean 'little Christs', and so being a follower of Christ was not as fashionable as it may be in our world today. In some instances people feared to be seen to be associating with Christ. Peter denying Christ is not such grand statement of reference to this fact. The reason was that the whole Jesus movement thing did not have the kind of acceptance you would expect them to have before the religious 'movers and shakers' of the day. And for that matter Peter was scared it would have meant being questioned alongside Jesus or even possibly being put to death. It should therefore take a lot in the day for this beggar to make a public submission to Jesus acknowledging his power to change his life.

The risk of submitting to Christ publicly

In the days of Jesus, He and His disciples were considered a sect. Jesus Christ in his days was not accepted as the Son of God. It was a huge risk and rather odd for a Jew who had a full access to the temple or the synagogue every day to decide to plea for mercy from a controversial figure as Jesus was considered by a section of the society at the time.

There was a possibility that one could be thrown out of the synagogue for following Christ. In spite of the potential hazards of associating with Christ openly and the potential of incurring the displeasure of the chiefs priests, the Pharisees, the Sadducees and the ardent believers of Judaism, he acknowledged the power that Christ possesses to ask for mercy and not just healing. It confirms how ready the visually challenged man was to face the backlash of the community in which he comes from. As a matter of possibility, this could also be one of the reasons Jesus stood still and spoke to him. That man was willing to let everything go; everything he could hold onto as a Jew. He was not afraid of what the people were going to say. He was more concerned about Jesus Christ giving him what he wanted than what other people will say. He was much bolder than Nicodemus who for fear of losing his position in the synagogue chose to meet Jesus at night. He feared to be seen with Jesus in broad daylight as his position in the synagogue could become untenable.

He chose self-preservation over potential public ridicule and the eventual decline of his reputation. There was a possibility that the visually challenged man might have thought to himself that he didn't have much to lose anyway or perhaps if he could see, he could even increase his chances for a better life someday. After all what has he got to lose? He would loose nothing if he could see he could do so much with his life in a longer term than the length of chastisement from the Jewish community opposed to Jesus. And that was worth more to him than the public opinion and a section of the public's display of disaffection towards him, which could be somehow temporary. He chose a much more permanent solution to his problem than a temporal one, and therefore also considered the risk associated with the decision to cry out to Jesus a temporal one. He was very sincere and open about what he wanted without any apologies. He had nothing to hide.

Another thing that is also worthy of mentioning in the above scripture in its application is that, we could come to Christ, and clothe ourselves in all kinds of things; business standing, family reputation, social status, public recognition and acclaim and achievements that makes it difficult for Christ to touch us. People portray themselves in a way that does not represent the real them. People sometimes make mistakes by pretending to be a people they are not. God cannot be conned. The bible says everything is naked before Him (Hebrews 4:13). The Lord appreciates coming to Him just as you are because He knows you anyway and see every situation you find yourself in. To come to God with big verbal expressions as though to make an impression on him to get Him to do for you what you want is not practical. There is nothing you can do to con God to do something for you. He is the Alpha and the Omega and the Omniscient God.

Sometimes going to God in tears in a way to emotionally blackmail Him does not work because He is above all that. Yes some humans can fall for it but not God. The explosion or expressions of emotions will not move God or will not push God to grant you your desires. All you need is to be able to come to God in the sincerity of your heart just as you are. Present yourselves as sincere as possible from the bottom of your heart and God will reach out to you. Jesus stood still and reached out to the man because he availed himself truly from his heart. He gave no thought to what the consequences of his action was. He was not concerned about what the Jewish were going to talk about. He recognised Jesus as the Christ and as someone who had the ability to heal him. For the visually challenged man that was his interest.

The condition for obtaining the mercy of God is simple, avail yourself and call upon the name of God. *"Call upon Me in the day of trouble; I will deliver you, and you shall glorify Me"* (Psalm 50:15). The Lord is more than willing to answer to your call for mercy or any other help you need from Him but it has to be from a very sincere and a pure heart. The Lord does not require you to do something superfluous in order to obtain His mercy. Paul the apostle writes even though I was once a blasphemer and a persecutor and a violent man, I was shown mercy because I acted in ignorance and unbelief, but for that reason I was shown mercy so that in me, the worst sinner, Christ Jesus might display his unlimited patience as an example for those who would believe on him and receive eternal life (I Timothy 1: 13 & 16).

Acknowledging the Jesus of History

It was amazing the level of faith that the beggar had. It would have been risky enough to openly declare one's faith in the supernatural ability of Jesus but to make something of Him, trying to locate Him within scripture as the son of David who had come to save mankind was even a much greater risk. The 'son of David' tag was not just a trace of the ancestry of Jesus Christ which was an undeniable fact but the usage of that term in that particular content of the statement of the visually challenged man was a reference to the prophesies in the Old Testament which refers to the root of the shoot of David who would sit on the throne in Israel – the description given of the Messiah and also Jesus being the Christ whose throne will be established forever (Isaiah 11:1; 2 Samuel 7:15-16). Considering the controversy about the identity of Christ in the public sphere and the consequence of an open declaration, which could possibly turn the hearts of some Jewish people, the man made that profound statement. The hearts of some Jewish people at the time could, through a further scrutiny of the statement in the light of scripture possibly come to follow Christ and that was a courageous thing to do. It was an incredible moment to openly declare him as the 'son of David', the Messiah of the human race in the ears of all who were present and for us in this present time.

We cannot dichotomise the humanity of Christ from His divinity in our understanding of Him. For us to be able to appreciate Him as saviour and to fully understand the salvific work on the cross for us, we need to have them harmonised in our understanding. Christ being divine alone could not have been enough to save us as He needed a body to live in as a human to go through what we go through to qualify according to the divine terms of engagement to buy us our salvation. Blood had to be shed for the propitiation of sin, and it could only take the blood of a holy human, since the blood of sheep and goats was not enough to buy the freedom of the human race once and for all and eternally. Therefore we need to fully understand Jesus and know Him from His humanity to His divinity to be able to fully appreciate His place in our lives. Our faith in Christ is further strengthened, knowing throughout the scriptures and not just by the experience that He is the Messiah. The scripture gives us the expectation of the experience through faith and the experience affirms the scriptures thus creating a body of truth about our experience with Christ.

The sad thing is that not many people are able to defend our faith from scriptural perspective not even to talk about the extrabiblical information that confirms certain historical events in scripture. We need to be astute students of the scriptures to understand for ourselves what we believe as the scriptures have it and not only from the perspective or interpretations of others. The experience of scriptures is not enough, and even the evidence of the truth of the scriptures in your life is not enough, you need to have the scriptural basis to defend your experience.

It is no coincidence that Paul advised Timothy to study to show himself approved as a workman who does not need to be ashamed but rightly diving the word of truth (2 Timothy 2:15). Timothy's approval was not only from the evidence of the scripture in his life but in his knowledge and correct interpretation of the scriptures. It is about time we take our bible studies seriously, and not only that but to equip ourselves with other study aids to help us to acquire knowledge of the scriptures, understand it, apply it, and be able to teach it to others. It is an affective way to consolidate our knowledge of God's word.

Jesus, the Saviour – Messiah who changes lives.

The visually challenged man's encounter with Jesus was life changing. His life changed totally from despair to a hope of a glorious future ahead of him. From our perspective as readers of the scriptures it was a life changing experience because we are informed and thought through that experience. It is not quite certain if that man knows we are inspired by his actions at this time. It might have been a private occurrence for him but it has a public and eternal significance to us now who read these texts. We are inspired and encouraged to emulate him. This is the impact his life and actions is having on us now and that in itself is a blessing and should be an eternally life changing experience for him since not all people are remembered in history for the right reasons. There are people in history that are remembered in the present to be reviled and cursed because of the negative impact their lives had on others.

The visually challenged man saw in Jesus a life transformer, but to Most of the Jews, He was just Jesus of Nazareth but to the blind beggar, He was the life-transforming Son of David. What the visually challenged beggar asked for was not for Jesus to show him compassion but asked for more beyond compassion to change his life completely. When even the people told him to shut up, he shouted louder. He knew his limitation and he knew Jesus was the right person who could deal with it. God sometimes uses the darkness of suffering to teach some people some valuable spiritual lessons. He is not the author of the dark situations we go through but He is able to use for our good both in the short term and in the long term. People sometimes must go through dark circumstances before they are able to see the mercy of God or change in their lives. In a similar instance to buttress the point I'm making now:

> "³ Jesus answered, "Neither this man nor his parents sinned, but that the works (mercy) of God should be revealed in him." (John 9:3)

God sometimes expects His people to grow into stronger persons as His redemptive purposes unfold in their situations. The ultimate goal of Jesus is to transform people's lives in the here and now and also eternally.

> "⁴⁰ So Jesus stood still and commanded him to be brought to Him. And when he had come near, He asked him, ⁴¹ saying, "What do you want Me to do for you?"
> He said, "Lord, that I may receive my sight." ⁴² Then Jesus said to him, "Receive your sight; your faith has

made you well."[43] *And immediately he received his sight, and followed Him, glorifying God. And all the people, when they saw it, gave praise to God." (Luke 18:40-43).*

The visually challenged man turned into a beggar, had his life transformed through faith in the mercy of Jesus.

The other cost of his condition

One painful experience can sometimes bring on other equally painful circumstances, and you can understand why the visually challenged man just didn't want to see. Due to the unfortunate situation of blindness and the lack of society's provision for their inclusion in society to live normal lives he resorted to begging. The blindness has caused him to assume another identity, which actually doesn't represent him in fairness. You can imagine how people in town, would refer to him as the blind beggar. His real identity as a person has been concealed in the misfortune that has befallen him. His real self has been overshadowed by the challenges that seem to have swamped him. Therefore crying out to Jesus was a cry for a total transformation of his life and certainly Jesus gave him that chance and opportunity. And that was just one of such examples of transformation that Jesus brought to those who had an encounter with Him. The excellent news is that He still transforms lives even today, when we cry out to him and give Him the chance to step into our lives.

Jesus came to make us see

When Jesus had come close to where that man sat he asked that, the visually challenged man be brought to Him. He then asked the man what he wanted Him (Jesus) to do for him? His response was that he wanted to see. Jesus touched him and he was able to see again. An interesting point to raise though about the visually challenged man was that he could see very well although he was physically blind. He had the ability to see in Christ, beyond the use of physical eyes, the total package he needed to transform his life. There is the likelihood that there may be others around Jesus who had some form of condition and needed some form of a remedy to their condition but didn't get it because probably they didn't see beyond what they might have heard Jesus has done in the lives of people and couldn't trust for something to create their own unique experience and story. We therefore need to see beyond, we need the eye of faith.

Again, unlike this visually challenged man, we may not be physically blind, and so we can even go through the usual practices expected of a Christian, yet, we can be blind spiritually. If we have the faith of the visually challenged man, then, we can allow Jesus to heal us totally. He will give us spiritual sight. With our ability to see spiritually, we will be able to recognise who Jesus really is in our lives, and having known Him, He will enable us prefer Him and the kingdom of God to all the worldly things. We will put aside values that secular society clings to and see as God wants us to see. With the power of the Spirit working in us, empowering us to listen to his words and act of them, we will follow him on the road to Jerusalem, accepting suffering and even death for the sake of the Gospel. The bible makes us to understand that the blind beggar had faith, which was expressed in action. The blind beggar 'saw' Jesus as the Messiah, Son of David, who could heal him from his blindness. It is an irony that the blind beggar could 'see' what the religious leaders failed to see. Jesus can heal you whether physically or spiritually, but you need to set aside anything that hinders you and come to Him and put your trust in Him. To see beyond the present is Wisdom, but to see beyond the possible is Faith. Through faith he saw the possibility of a transformed life, and that enabled him to physically see Jesus. Jesus came to not only to deal with physical blindness but also with spiritual blindness. Many Christians today are spiritually blind. We are called to see and follow Him.

Jesus came to create opportunity

Sometimes, those of us who have the abilities to read, hear, walk and do all kinds of life activities do not take the opportunity when the message of God comes to us. The blind man has only heard of Jesus, the son of David yet he made his request from Him when the opportunity came his way. We must know that blind beggar heard what the mercy of God can do in his life which made him ask for mercy. Jesus of Nazareth is passing by. For the blind man, there was no concept of I'm leaving this until next week or next year. "I will think about it and get back to you". Jesus is passing by and wants to deal with your situation now. Not maybe next year. If the man had waited there would not have been a next week or next year. This was an opportunity Jesus was giving the people of Jericho to experience His personal presence and the mercy of Him. And He was quite prepared to stop and deal with people's limitations - the blind man. The blind beggar never said the people were many or he wants to wait for Jesus when He returns from His Journey. He took the opportunity that came to him; he never procrastinated it or made anything to distract him of the opportunity. Whenever you come before God, He is challenging you that all your sufferings, depressions and worries Jesus is passing by and wants to deal with them. You need mercy. There is no-one that does not need it. Let's therefore come boldly to the throne of grace to receive what we need. "Let us therefore come boldly to the throne of grace, that we may obtain mercy and find grace to help in time of need"(Hebrews 4:16)

Furthermore, the blind beggar believing that Jesus could do the above in his life made him to cried out "...*Jesus, Son of David, have mercy on me.*" His conviction was however based on the Old Testament understanding of mercy. The Old Testament understanding of mercy was base on the sacrifices made at the Mercy seat in the Ark of the Covenant.

Chapter Three

ENTER THE HOLY OF HOLIES -
THE PLACE OF MERCY

We have discussed already that the visually challenged man was not an ardent follower of Christ and his only encounter with Christ is what we have been exploring. The man was a Jew with Judaism as his religion as most Jews at the time were. It was not surprising therefore his knowledge of the Scriptures gave him an understanding to locate Jesus within written history, the scriptures, and therefore referred to him as 'son of David'. Because of his leaning towards the Old Testament, his call to Jesus to show him mercy was not from the New Testament understanding of mercy, which in some sense may mean the expression of compassion and love in tangible ways. His cry for mercy was from the Old Testament perspective. Those that recorded this event wrote in Greek as the visually challenged called out to Jesus but there should be an understanding in His mind as the bedrock of his request which went beyond just being shown compassion and love as we currently understand mercy to mean.

Therefore there is the need for us to explore from the Old Testament what the word mercy mean. The pattern of God's dealings with people in the Old Testament, at the core of which is mercy, also provides the framework to understanding his dealings in the New Testament. God desires a relationship with humankind, but must show mercy to them in order for this relationship to be built. Of course, the New Testament expounds the theme of God's mercy in the light of Christ. Before then we would look at it from the perspective of the Old Testament.

The word mercy gains prominence from the mercy seat, which was situated, or an essential component of the Ark of the Covenant. The Ark of the Covenant was situated in the Holy of Holies of the tabernacle. To elucidate better the concept of the Mercy seat we have to look at the tabernacle and the various components present to appreciate the essence of the mercy seat and its significance in the lives of the worshippers. Every component, equipment, and objects and vessels in the tabernacle are supposed to be working together towards the provision of Mercy. It would also help us to be able to correctly apply the information and understanding we obtain from the mercy seat to our lives today, as we see in later chapters.

The gate of the tabernacle

The first feature of the tabernacle is that, it had only one gate by which people could enter into the tabernacle courtyard. The gate was about 30 feet wide. It was located directly in the centre of the outer court on the east end. A curtain covered the gate or screen made of finely twisted linen in blue, purple and scarlet. The one and only gate is a representation of Christ as the only way through which one could obtain mercy and subsequently qualify to fellowship with God and worship Him. To do this, one must enter in through the gate to the place where God dwelled. Jesus in the declaration of his identity, made a few "I am" statements:

> [6] *Jesus said to him, "I am the way, the truth, and the life. No one comes to the Father except through Me."* **(John 14:6)**

"⁹ I am the door. If anyone enters by Me, he will be saved, and will go in and out and find pasture." **(John 10:9)**

He also said:

"Enter by the narrow gate; for wide is the gate and broad is the way that leads to destruction, and there are many who go in by it. ¹⁴ Because narrow is the gate and difficult is the way which leads to life, and there are few who find it." **(Matthew 7:13-14)**

The act of entering the gate to the tabernacle was significant to the Israelites. By entering, one could find mercy of God through forgiveness of sin and fellowship with God. Those who did not repent were not entering this "narrow way."

The Brazen Altar

The second feature of the tabernacle was the brazen altar or bronze altar, or altar of sacrifice which was situated right inside the courtyard upon entering the gate to the tabernacle. The Hebrew root for altar means "to slay" or "slaughter." The Latin word *alta* means "high." The altar was a "high place for sacrifice or slaughter." The altar stood raised on a mound of earth, higher than its surrounding furniture. This is a projection of Christ, our sacrifice, lifted up on the cross, His altar, which stood on a hill called Golgotha. The altar was the place for burning animal sacrifices. It showed the Israelites that the first step for a sinful man to obtain mercy from the holy God was to be cleansed by the blood of an innocent creature. For a sin offering, a person had to bring an animal — a male one without blemish or defect from the flock or herd — to the priest at the tabernacle gate.

> "⁴ *Then he shall put his hand on the head of the burnt offering, and it will be accepted on his behalf to make atonement for him."* (**Leviticus 1:4**)

By laying their hand upon the head of the offering, the person was identifying with the sacrifice. His sin and guilt was being transferred from them to the animal. The priest would then slaughter the animal, sprinkle its blood in front of the veil of the Holy Place, burn the sacrifice, and pour the rest of it at the bottom of the altar. Blood is a significant agent of atonement and cleansing in the Old Testament. It is a sign that the merciful God has accepted the cry of the weak.

> *"11 For the life of the flesh is in the blood, and I have given it to you upon the altar to make atonement for your souls; for it is the blood that makes atonement for the soul."* **(Leviticus 17:11)**

> *"22 And according to the law almost all things are purified with blood, and without shedding of blood there is no remission."* **(Hebrews 9:22)**

Although the blood of the sacrifices covered the sins of the Israelites, they had to perform the sacrifices year after year, for they were not freed permanently of a guilty conscience. However, Jesus Christ, the Lamb of God, came as the ultimate and last sacrifice for mankind when He offered up His life. As Isaiah prophesied, the Christ would be like a lamb that is led to the slaughter and pierced for our transgressions. His blood was sprinkled and poured out at the cross for us.

The Bible says much about this:

> *"And He said to them, "This is My blood of the new covenant, which is shed for many." (Mark 14:24) " knowing that you were not redeemed with corruptible things, like silver or gold, from your aimless conduct received by tradition from your fathers, [19] but with the precious blood of Christ, as of a lamb without blemish and without spot."* **(1 Peter 1:18-19)**

"¹³ For if the blood of bulls and goats and the ashes of a heifer, sprinkling the unclean, sanctifies for the purifying of the flesh, ¹⁴ how much more shall the blood of Christ, who through the eternal Spirit offered Himself without spot to God, cleanse your conscience from dead works to serve the living God?"
(Hebrews 9:13-14)

"We have been made holy through the sacrifice of the body of Jesus Christ once for all. …By one sacrifice he has made perfect forever those who are being made holy. …And where these have been forgiven, there is no longer any sacrifice for sin." **(Hebrews 10:10, 14, 18)**

"For He made Him who knew no sin to be sin for us, that we might become the righteousness of God in Him."
(2 Corinthians 5:21)

The Laver

The third feature of the tabernacle was the laver, or a basin, was a large bowl filled with water located halfway between the brazen altar and the Holy Place. Although the bible did not give the specific measurements for the Laver, it was to be made entirely of bronze. The priests were to wash their hands and their feet in it before entering the Holy Place.

The priests also cleansed themselves at the laver before serving in the Holy Place, so that they would be pure and not die before a holy God. After washing their hands and feet at the laver, the priests could enter the Holy Place, which was the first room in the tent of the tabernacle. There were three pieces of furniture in the Holy Place: the menorah, the table of showbread and the golden altar of incense.

This feature of the tabernacle, the menorah, also called the "golden lamp stand" or "candlestick," stood at the left side of the

Holy Place. It was hammered out of one piece of pure gold. Like for the laver, there were no specific instructions about the size of the menorah, but the fact that it was fashioned out of one piece of pure gold would have limited its size.

The lamp stand had a central branch from which three branches extended from each side, forming a total of seven branches. Seven lamps holding olive oil and wicks stood on top of the branches. Each branch looked like that of an almond tree, containing buds, blossoms and flowers. The priests were instructed to keep the lamps burning continuously.

"Then the Lord spoke to Moses, saying: ² "Command the children of Israel that they bring to you pure oil of pressed olives for the light, to make the lamps burn continually. ³ Outside the veil of the Testimony, in the tabernacle of meeting, Aaron shall be in charge of

it from evening until morning before the Lord continually; it shall be a statute forever in your generations."
(Leviticus 24:1-3)

The two significant symbols that can be seen from include the fact that it was made of pure gold and had seven branches. Pure gold is a representation of the deity and perfection of Jesus Christ, and seven is the number of completeness in the Bible. The believer is made complete by the perfection of Christ in one's life.

The Table of Showbread

Another feature of the tabernacle is the table of showbread which is a small table made of acacia wood and overlaid with pure gold. It stood on the right side of the Holy Place across from the lamp stand and held 12 loaves of bread, representing the 12 tribes of Israel. The priests baked the bread with fine flour and it remained on the table before the Lord for a week; every Sabbath day the priests would remove it and eat it in the Holy Place, then put fresh bread on the table. Only priests could eat the bread, and it could only be eaten in the Holy Place, because it was holy.

One other feature of the tabernacle was the golden altar of incense, which sat in front of the curtain that separated the Holy Place from the Holy of Holies. This altar was smaller than the brazen altar. It was made of acacia wood and overlaid with pure gold. Four horns protruded from the four corners of the altar.

God commanded the priests to burn incense on the golden altar every morning and evening, the same time that the daily burnt offerings were made. The incense was to be left burning continually throughout the day and night as a pleasing aroma to the Lord. It was made of an equal part of four precious spices (stacte, onycha, galbanum and frankincense) and was considered holy.

God commanded the Israelites not to use the same formula outside the tabernacle to make perfume for their own consumption; otherwise, they were to be cut off from their people.

> "³⁴ And the Lord said to Moses: "Take sweet spices, stacte and onycha and galbanum, and pure frankincense with these sweet spices; there shall be equal amounts of each. ³⁵ You shall make of these an incense, a compound according to the art of the perfumer, salted, pure, and holy. ³⁶ And you shall beat some of it very fine, and put some of it before the Testimony in the tabernacle of meeting where I will meet with you. It shall be most holy to you. ³⁷ But as for the incense which you shall make, you shall not make any for yourselves, according to its composition. It shall be to you holy for the Lord. ³⁸ Whoever makes any like it, to smell it, he shall be cut off from his people." **(Exodus 30:34-38)**

The incense was a symbol of the prayers and intercession of the people going up to God as a sweet fragrance. God wanted His dwelling to be a place where people could approach Him and pray to Him so He could release his mercy on His children.

"…for my house will be called a house of prayer for all nations." (Isaiah 56:7)

The picture of prayers wafting up to heaven like incense is captured in David's psalm and also in John's vision in Revelations:

"Let my prayer be set before You as incense, The lifting up of my hands as the evening sacrifice" **(Psalm 141:2)**

"Then another angel, having a golden censer, came and stood at the altar. He was given much incense, that he should offer it with the prayers of all the saints upon the golden altar which was before the throne. ⁴ And the smoke of the

incense, with the prayers of the saints, ascended before God from the angel's hand." (Revelations 8:3-4)

The Horns of the Golden Altar

The horns of the golden altar were sprinkled with blood from the animal sacrifice to cleanse and purify it from the sins of the Israelites (Leviticus 4:7, 16:18). Just as the horns on the brazen altar represent the power of Christ's blood to forgive sins, the horns on golden altar signify the power of Jesus' blood in prayer as we confess our sins and ask for mercy.

"15 And the prayer of faith will save the sick, and the Lord will raise him up. And if he has committed sins, he will be forgiven. 16 Confess your trespasses[a] to one another, and pray for one another, that you may be healed. The effective, fervent prayer of a righteous man avails much." **(James 5:15-16)**

Horns symbolised power and strength in biblical times. When the sacrifice was made, blood was dabbed on the horns of the altar, signifying the power of the blood to atone for sins. In the same way, there is mighty power in the blood of Christ. Jesus is the "horn of our salvation" (Psalm 18:2, Luke 1:69). The animal sacrifices bore reference to the Passover lambs, which the Israelites slaughtered in like manner to save their firstborns from the last plague of God's judgment on Egypt (Exodus 12:1-13). Similarly, as the Passover lambs were eaten after they were slaughtered, some of the sacrificial lambs also were eaten. Just as the sacrificial lambs were sacrificed and eaten, so Jesus' body was sacrificed and "eaten." It was no coincidence that on the night before the Passover when Jesus was crucified, He "took bread, gave thanks and broke it, and gave it to his disciples, saying, 'Take and eat; this is my body'" (Matthew 26:26). Earlier Jesus had taught His disciples:

"[53] Then Jesus said to them, "Most assuredly, I say to you, unless you eat the flesh of the Son of Man and drink His blood, you have no life in you. [54] Whoever eats My flesh and drinks My blood has eternal life, and I will raise him up at the last day. [55] For My flesh is food indeed, and My blood is drink indeed. [56] He who eats My flesh and drinks My blood abides in Me, and I in him." **(John 6:53-56)**

Jesus Himself is the Lamb of God as well as the Passover Lamb for those who believe in Him.

The Ark of the Testimony

10 "And they shall make an ark of acacia wood; two and a half cubits shall be its length, a cubit and a half its width, and a cubit and a half its height. 11 And you shall overlay it with pure gold, inside and out you shall overlay it, and shall make on it a molding of gold all around. 12 You shall cast four rings of gold for it, and put them in its four corners; two rings shall be on one side, and two rings on the other side. 13 And you shall make poles of acacia wood, and overlay them with gold. 14 You shall put the poles into the rings on the sides of the ark, that the ark may be carried by them. 15 The poles shall be in the rings of the ark; they shall not be taken from it. 16 And you shall put into the ark the Testimony which I will give you.

17 "You shall make a mercy seat of pure gold; two and a half cubits shall be its length and a cubit and a half its width. 18 And you shall make two cherubim of gold; of hammered work you shall make them at the two ends of the mercy seat. 19 Make one cherub at one end, and the other cherub at the other end; you shall make the cherubim at the two ends of it of one piece with the mercy seat. 20 And the cherubim shall stretch out their wings above, covering the mercy seat with their wings, and they shall face one another; the faces of the cherubim shall be toward the mercy seat. 21 You shall put the mercy seat on top of the ark, and in the ark you shall put the Testimony that I will give you.22 And there I will meet with you, and I will speak with you from above the mercy seat, from between the two cherubim which are on the ark of the Testimony, about everything which I will give you in commandment to the children of Israel.

The Table for the Showbread

23 "You shall also make a table of acacia wood; two cubits shall be its length, a cubit its width, and a cubit and a half its height. 24 And you shall overlay it with pure gold, and make a molding of gold all around. 25 You shall make for it a frame of a handbreadth all around, and you shall make a gold molding for the frame all around. 26 And you shall make for it four rings of gold, and put the rings on the four corners that are at its four legs. 27 The rings shall be close to the frame, as holders for the poles to bear the table. 28 And you shall make the poles of acacia wood, and overlay them with gold, that the table may be carried with them. 29 You shall make its dishes, its pans, its pitchers, and its bowls for pouring. You shall make them of pure gold. 30 And you shall set the showbread on the table before Me always.

The Gold Lamp stand

31 "You shall also make a lamp stand of pure gold; the lamp stand shall be of hammered work. Its shaft, its branches, its bowls, its ornamental knobs, and flowers shall be of one piece. 32 And six branches shall come out of its sides: three branches of the lamp stand out of one side, and three branches of the lamp stand out of the other side. 33 Three bowls shall be made like almond blossoms on one

branch, with an ornamental knob and a flower, and three bowls made like almond blossoms on the other branch, with an ornament al knob and a flower – and so for the six branches that come out of the lamp stand. 34 On the lamp stand itself four bowls shall be made like almond blossoms, each with its ornamental knob and flower. 35 And there shall be a knob under the first two branches of the same, a knob under the second two branches of the same, and a knob under the third two branches of the same, according to the six branches that extend from the lamp stand. 36 Their knobs and their branches shall be of one piece; all of it shall be one hammered piece of pure gold. 37 You shall make seven lamps for it, and they shall arrange its lamps so that they give light in front of it. 38 And its wick-trimmers and their trays shall be of pure gold. 39 It shall be made of a talent of pure gold, with

all these utensils. 40 And see to it that
you make them according to the pattern
which was shown you on the mountain."
(Exodus 25:1-40)

The Ark of the Covenant

In this chapter, we will look at how the tabernacle was built, its representation and how it relates to the mercy of God on which the people of the God received mercy. During the time of the Israelites, the mercy of God could be experienced at the *Mercy Seat* in the tabernacle of God. It was the only sacred place where God dwelled. The tabernacle was made upon divine instruction and it mirrors God's passion to redeem man from sin under the old covenant. The Hebrew word *mishkan* is translated "Tabernacle" and means "tent" or "place of dwelling." It was a sacred place where God chose to meet His people, the Israelites, during the 40 years they wandered in the desert under Moses' leadership. It was the only place the people of Israel could seek the Mercy. This sacred place that housed the presence of God was mirrored as Christ in the New Testament, because Christ was the embodiment of God on earth. He was fully God and fully human.

> [10] *"And they shall make an ark of acacia wood; two and a half cubits shall be its length, a cubit and a half its width, and a cubit and a half its height.* [11] *And you shall overlay it with pure gold, inside and out you shall overlay it, and shall make on it a molding of gold all around.* [12] *You shall cast four rings of gold for it, and put them in its four corners; two rings shall be on one side, and two rings on the other side.* [13] *And you shall make poles of acacia wood, and overlay them with gold.* [14] *You shall put the poles into the rings on the sides of the ark, that the ark may be carried by them.* [15] *The poles shall be in the rings of the ark; they shall not*

be taken from it. ¹⁶ And you shall put into the ark the Testimony which I will give you.

¹⁷ "You shall make a mercy seat of pure gold; two and a half cubits shall be its length and a cubit and a half its width. ¹⁸ And you shall make two cherubim of gold; of hammered work you shall make them at the two ends of the mercy seat. ¹⁹ Make one cherub at one end, and the other cherub at the other end; you shall make the cherubim at the two ends of it of one piece with the mercy seat. ²⁰ And the cherubim shall stretch out their wings above, covering the mercy seat with their wings, and they shall face one another; the faces of the cherubim shall be toward the mercy seat. ²¹ You shall put the mercy seat on top of the ark, and in the ark you shall put the Testimony that I will give you. ²² And there I will meet with you, and I will speak with you from above

the mercy seat, from between the two cherubim which are on the ark of the Testimony, about everything which I will give you in commandment to the children of Israel."
(Exodus 25:10-22)

The above scriptural passage gives a description of the Ark. It symbolizes the presence of God in the children of Israel. In the past, God used to rule the people directly. This was called theocracy. In other words, God was the president or the prime minister of the people. At that time, God was their only leader who steers the affairs of how they should live on earth. If they needed to do anything, they have to ask from God in the tabernacle. The Ark of the Covenant was very important as far as the worship and their relationship with God were concerned because the Ark professed the faith of the people of Israel, the Merciful God. The ark of the Covenant also represented the government of the people, being God Himself. But prior to the building of the Ark, the people did not know how to plea on such mercy of God. That is why even after creation, when God told Adam and Eve not to eat the forbidden fruit and they ate, God made an animal skin for them to cover their nakedness because of mercy. However at this time in the era of Adam and Eve although God exercised mercy in His dealings with His people, such as the example of covering them with an animal skin, mercy have not as yet been institutionalised in the worship of his people and it was the ark of the covenant which carried the mercy seat that accomplished this.

The people of God might have known God operated on the basis of mercy but prior to the building of the Ark of the Covenant; mercy was not yet institutionalized in the worship of the people of Israel. There were things in the Ark that were to remind the people of Israel, of God's miraculous deliverance for them. When the Ark was completed, it was placed in the holy of holies. Whenever it was time for the high priest to offer the sacrifices of atonement, which was usually once a year, an animal is killed and the blood is poured on the mercy seat of the Ark of the Covenant. When the blood touches the seat, the Israelites get to know that their sins have been forgiven or there has been atonement for their sins.

In those days, before the high priest offers such sacrifice, usually there were sections in the tabernacle; the holy of holies, the holy place, the court of men, the court of women and the court of Gentiles and the strangers. The sacrifices take place at the holy place where the priest removes his cloth and puts on a new cloth which has small bells at the hem. When the people who have come to the tabernacle to worship hear those bells, they get the signal that the high priest is about to make a sacrifice. The high priest waist is usually tied with a very thick rope in case he is struck dead, he would be drawn out of the holy of holies to the court of men to be carried and buried without the people in the court getting in the holy of holies or even touching the mercy seat because it was abominable for any calibre of person to go inside.

After the sacrifice, the special clothing the priest put on for the sacrifice of the priest is taken off. The bells at the hem of the priest's clothing make noise for a second time to signify that Jehovah God has accepted the sacrifice. The people will make a loud noise to commemorate the acceptance of the sacrifice. In the same way, when Jesus died and rose from the dead, some of the disciples wanted to touch Him but He told them he has not yet shown Himself to His father. He did not allow anyone to touch him after his resurrection because he has to see his father first. He eventually ascended to heaven and as the disciples were gathered and in one accord; singing and praising the Name of the most high God, suddenly they heard a sound of a rushing wind in the room, they saw a cloves of fire on their heads and began to speak in tongues. This experience on the day of Pentecost empowered the disciples to go out and preach the gospel.

What Jesus wanted to put across was that He wanted to see his father or himself as a sacrifice. The blood that Jesus offered on the cross at Calvary has to go to the heavenly place for it to be accepted by God so that mankind can have their freedom. That is why after Jesus went to his father in heaven, his disciples received the power to do much greater works that they never thought. This is because his blood has reached the mercy seat.

As it used to happen in the Old Testament, the people in the court must hear the bell for the second time as a proof that mercy has been released and hence their sins have been forgiven by Jehovah God.

Likewise at the time of Jesus, he has to show himself to God as He claimed upon meeting some of the disciples who wanted to touch him after His resurrection. Having accomplished shown Himself to the father after the sacrifice on the cross at Calvary for the mercy of God to be released unto his disciples and all mankind.

In that and many other ways, as we will see, the tabernacle really was a prophetic projection of the Lord's redemptive plan for His people. The tabernacle became the embodiment of God's presence and government among His people.

> "³ And I heard a loud voice from heaven saying, "Behold, the tabernacle of God is with men, and He will dwell with them, and they shall be His people. God Himself will be with them and be their God." *(Revelation 21:3)*

This embodiment of God (Tabernacle) had different feature which had their respective meanings to the people of Israel and all generations after. In the New Testament, John writes: *"And the Word became flesh and dwelt among us, and we beheld His glory, the glory as of the only begotten of the Father, full of grace and truth."* (John 1:14) This word "dwell" is the same word for "tabernacle" in the Old Testament. In other words, God came in a totally human form to *dwell* or to *tabernacle* among His people. As He walked upon the earth and lived among the Jews, Jesus Christ Himself fulfilled the picture of the Old Testament tabernacle which was revelation of God's mercy to mankind.

Let us look at some special features of the tabernacle used in the Old Testament and what they symbolise.

Mercy - The foundation of God's Covenant with Humans

Mercy is the foundation of God's covenant. In this relationship, mercy then comes to be seen as the quality in God that directs him to forge a relationship with people who absolutely do not deserve to be in a relationship with Him. Mercy is generally manifested in God's activity on behalf of his people to free them from slavery; it is neither theory nor principle. As the passages taken up with the establishment of the covenant with Israel show, God's mercy is a driving force in leading Him to create a relationship with human-kind adopting Israel as model to exhibit this quality in His dealings with all who believe in Him and desire to forge a relationship with him.

We will delve into the mercy seat on which the blood of the lamb was poured for the atonement of people's sins. The mercy seat of the Ark of Covenant that was housed in the tabernacle was a replica of what existed in heaven – a shadow or model on earth of what actually existed in heaven. It was on the mercy seat in heaven that Jesus made His sacrifice for all humankind once and for all. The Ark of God in the tabernacle now only exist in heaven, after Christ's sacrifice and the curtain torn apart to declare redundant the use of the ark in the temple. And as already explained it was on that mercy seat in heaven, Jesus poured his blood and consequently sounds from heaven was recognised as a sign of the acceptance of His sacrifice in heaven on behalf of all human-kind. This manifestation on earth took the form already mentioned in the earlier paragraph. And it seems as though the disciples understood this occurrence quite well considering the sermon of peter to the gentiles and Jews who had gathered in Jerusalem on that day. The mercy seat has existed since time immemorial, considering the fact that God showed Moses a replica of every aspect of the tabernacle and in addition gave him the dimensions and measurements to build the model. It couldn't have been that the tabernacle might have been created upon Christ's death to make room for that sacrifice to be received in heaven.

"Offerings for the Sanctuary Then the Lord spoke to Moses, saying: 2 "Speak to the children of Israel, that they bring Me an offering. From everyone who gives it willingly with his heart you shall take My offering. 3 And this is the offering which you shall take from them: gold, silver, and bronze; 4 blue, purple, and scarlet thread, fine linen, and goats' hair; 5 ram skins dyed red, badger skins, and acacia wood;6 oil for the light, and spices for the anointing oil and for the sweet incense;7 onyx stones, and stones to be set in the ephod and in the breastplate. 8 And let them make Me a sanctuary, that I may dwell among them. 9 According to all that I show you, that is, the pattern of the tabernacle

and the pattern of all its furnishings,
just so you shall make it.

That is why the blind man said Jesus have Mercy on me. It is through this sacrifice on the mercy seat that forgiveness and reconciliation were made possible among the Israelites because the blood sacrifice that was sprinkled upon the *Mercy Seat* once a year was a propitiation or atonement for their sins. The root word for *Mercy Seat* or "Atonement Cover" is a Hebrew word that is spelled, "*kaphar*" or written *kaporet,* which means: To cover; to make atonement or reconcile; to appease, placate, cancel, or annul and finally; to cleanse, forgive, pardon, purge away or put off. It suggests the idea of obliterating the properties and characteristics of an element to make it unrecognizable or to lose its very essence. By implication there is a total *wipe out* and *restoration to the original* when mercy comes into contact with any element. These concepts would be fully explored in separate chapters later. It is at the *Mercy Seat* that man's sin is annulled and completely obliterated by the blood and restored to the original state. And not just sin, but a life can be restored to its original state after certain situations and circumstances have been reviewed by the working power of the blood. It is there that God makes atonement for that sin and reconciles man to Him. Similar to you, what would you do when you reconcile your chequebook and realise there was a debt owed by humankind that he could not pay. He had "written cheques" on his relationship with God when there was nothing in that account to cover the cheques. Mankind had not made any deposit in his "sin debt account" to offset the debt. Mankind had sold the only valuable thing that he possessed that could be used as collateral. He had sold his eternal soul to the devil in exchange for an eternity without God. Needless to say, mankind got the worst end of the deal. Not only could he never repay his debt, but the debt, with penalties and interest, on top of more penalties and interest, just continued to grow and drive man deeper into slavery to sin and of dominion of Satan.

At the *Mercy Seat*, the payment for that debt was made, not by man, but by God, for God only could give something that was worthwhile as repayment for our debt of sin. In effect, God covered our "worthless cheques"; He paid the debt we owed; and He redeemed, or bailed us out of our jail of slavery to sin and the devil; and He then signed over all that Heaven has to us as joint heirs to His only Son, Jesus Christ. He cancelled our debt of sin with His own blood upon the *Mercy Seat*. The Holy Spirit then became the guarantee of the freedom from that debt when we receive Him into our lives, after our debt is paid and thereafter cleansed. By paying our debt with His own blood, Jesus fulfilled all of the requirements of the Law that were on our record. Then

He blotted out the ink of that record and expunged any and all charges against us, cancelling the death penalty, annulling the convictions and sentencing as passed by the Law, and appeased the requirements of a Holy God by simply saying three little words, "I Forgive You"!

"and you are complete in Him, who is the head of all principality and power.
Not Legalism but Christ
[11] In Him you were also circumcised with the circumcision made without hands, by putting off the body of the sins of the flesh, by the circumcision of Christ,[12] buried with Him in baptism, in which you also were raised with Him through faith in the working of God, who raised Him from the dead. [13] And you, being dead in your trespasses and the uncircumcision of your flesh, He has made alive together with Him, having forgiven you all trespasses, [14] having wiped out the handwriting of

requirements that was against us, which was contrary to us. And He has taken it out of the way, having nailed it to the cross." **(Colossians 2:10-14)**

We must know that under the New Testament, the mercy of God in the tabernacle in the olden days has now become our body by faith in Christ Jesus. The reason it is so is because the scriptures says we are the temples of the Holy Spirit. When people accept Jesus and they invite Him into their lives, their bodies become the temple of God. We are temples of God because we have been born again in a Spiritual way. This time, our sins are not forgiven at the mercy seat as it was happening annually in the old tabernacle but now by faith through the sacrifice of Jesus on the cross and maintaining the connection to the cross.

"There was a man of the Pharisees named Nicodemus, a ruler of the Jews.[2] This man came to Jesus by night and said to Him, "Rabbi, we know that You are a teacher come from God; for no one can do these signs that You do unless God is with him."

[3] Jesus answered and said to him, "Most assuredly, I say to you, unless one is born again, he cannot see the kingdom of God."

[4] Nicodemus said to Him, "How can a man be born when he is old? Can he enter a second time into his mother's womb and be born?"

[5] Jesus answered, "Most assuredly, I say to you, unless one is born of water and the Spirit, he cannot enter the kingdom of God. [6] That which is born of the flesh is flesh, and that which is born of the Spirit is spirit. [7] Do not marvel that I said to you, 'You must be born again."
(John 3:1-7)

We are temples of God because we are glorifying God in our bodies and in our spirits.

"19 Or do you not know that your body is the temple of the Holy Spirit who is in you, whom you have from God, and you are not your own? 20 For you were bought at a price; therefore glorify God in your body and in your spirit, which are God's." **(1 Corinthians 6:19-20)**

"'Heaven is My throne, And earth is My footstool. What house will you build for Me? says the Lord, Or what is the place of My rest?" **(Acts 7:49)**

Man was created to be the house of God, His resting place. The plan of redemption proceeds on its course until we become the eternal tabernacle of God. While the *Mercy Seat* served as an important part of Jewish worship during the tabernacle and temple periods, the coming of Jesus

Christ has brought with it a new covenant by which each person can find atonement or forgiveness and payment for their sins through faith in Jesus Christ as God's risen Son (John 3:16;Ephesians 2:8-9).

The *Mercy Seat* points to the person of Jesus Christ. The *Mercy Seat* is a beautiful picture of the work of the Lord Jesus Christ; what Jesus came into this world to do for you and me - His workmanship. Jesus Christ became the substitute for the animals that were killed for the atonement of sins in the Old Testament.

Chapter Four

MERCY IN THE GENERAL CONTEXT OF SCRIPTURE

"He has shown you, O man, what is good;
And what does the Lord require of you
But to do justly, To love mercy, And to
walk humbly with your God?"
(Micah 6:8)

Mercy is a fundamental part of Christian life. By understanding the mercy of God, you will be able to understand better the passionate love of Christ for each of us, even though we may be sinners. Through mercy, we can see the teachings of Christ in a clearer way and become aware of the truth and see the power in the mercy. It is mercy that leads us to the truth. It helps us to see beyond the barriers that come between us and the love and mercy of Christ. Christ reveals the mercy of God to us. We allow Christ to manifest Himself to others, through us, when we are merciful.

The first example of mercy in Scripture was in the Garden of Eden. When Adam sinned, he and Eve were justly deserving of instant death. Instead, God allowed them to live and procreate so that they and their posterity might learn both the goodness and seriousness of the Word that proceeds out of the mouth of God, and the ultimate result of sin. The first use of the word "mercy" in Scripture is found in Genesis 19:19 concerning Lot and the destruction of the cities of Sodom and Gomorrah. Zoar, which was one of these cities, was not destroyed because of Lot's request to flee from the impending disaster and hide there. The mercy of God toward Lot was demonstrated when the angels took him and his family by the hand and led them away to safety.

Ever since, God has been teaching the concept of mercy to humans by His own example, as well as the other examples of biblical characters, He reveals in the scriptures. Through His mercy, the human creation has been subjected to the rigour of labouring to provide sustenance: so that they would have less time for evil pursuits and the degradation of mans standing with God, which such evil pursuit bring. Human-kind has not only escaped the consequences of neither sin nor the accompanying degradation, but has also had the opportunity to see the exercise of mercy and its results in the lives of others in scripture.

"2 that the sons of God saw the daughters of men, that they were beautiful; and

they took wives for themselves of all whom they chose. ³ And the Lord said, "My Spirit shall not strive with man forever, for he is indeed flesh; yet his days shall be one hundred and twenty years." (Genesis 6:2-3).

David was a man who committed a multitude of sins, yet, when he realised he had sinned against God, David came before God with a repentant heart, he was forgiven. This shows how gracious and merciful God had been to David in appointing him king over the nation, saving his life, and giving him the pleasures of life. In Scripture, the word "mercy" is used more in the Book of Psalms than anywhere else.

The first occurrence in that book is Psalm 4:

*"Hear me when I call, O God of my righteousness: thou has enlarged me when I was in distress; have **mercy** upon me, and hear my prayer"* **(Psalm 4:1).**

Many of the examples of mercy given in God's word do not use the exact word *mercy*. But in the narratives, we see the act and its characteristics. Mercy is an act motivated by compassion, sympathy, and love.

> "And the LORD passed before him and proclaimed, "The LORD, the LORD God, merciful and gracious, longsuffering, and abounding in goodness and truth."
> **(Exodus 34:6)**

Mercy is compassion or forbearance shown to an offender. Charity, clemency, grace and leniency are synonyms and usually have some of the same elements as mercy. However, mercy implies compassion that forebears punishment even when justice calls for it. Both the Hebrew and Greek words from which mercy is translated give the same tenor of thought as the dictionary definition. Underlying the practice of mercy is a feeling of sympathy and compassion for the plight of others, and a desire to relieve their distress. Having a heart willing to listen to the plight of others, and a willingness to remedy the problem if possible, is a basic requirement for one who wishes to be merciful and thereby receive the mercy promised by our master (Matthew 5:7).

According to the Blue Letter Bible, the word "mercy", in the King James translation (KJV), occurs 276 times in 261 verses. God's mercy is shown so many times in the Bible and in our own lives we often fail to see it. If you would do a concordance check of this word, you will see that God's mercy abounds. His mercy could even be inferred throughout the Bible even when the actual word, "mercy", is not in the passage. In the Hebrew Language, mercy comes from the word *rahamin*. The scripture that encapsulate its meaning in an example is

> *"Can a woman forget her nursing child, And not have compassion on the son of her womb? Surely they may forget, Yet I will not forget you."* **(Isaiah 49:15).**

The mercy of God is one of His attributes that exists only for His children. That is to say, in order to display mercy, it is necessary that there first be misery.

In Jesus' Sermon on the Mount, our Lord began by contrasting the difference between dealing with one's friends and one's enemies. He said if we do good to those who do good to us, if we lend to those whom we know will pay us back, and if we love those who love us, we are no better than the world who do the same things. He said:

> *"But love your enemies, do good, and lend, hoping for nothing in return; and your reward will be great, and you will be sons of the Most High. For He is kind to the unthankful and evil. Therefore be merciful, just as your Father also is merciful."* **(Luke 6:35, 36).**

Here is Jesus' definition of mercy: being kind to the unthankful and those who are evil.

God treats those who are unappreciative and those of an evil disposition better than they deserve. He goes beyond strict justice and treats creatures better than they could claim as their just due. It is out of this sheer mercy that we are admonished to do the same. It was out of mercy that Jesus redeemed the child with the demon.

"LORD, HAVE MERCY ON MY SON, for he is an epileptic and suffers severely; for he often falls into the fire and often into the water...... And Jesus rebuked the demon, and it came out of him; AND THE CHILD WAS CURED FROM THAT VERY HOUR." (Matthew 17:15, 18)

It was out of mercy of Jesus and the faith of the woman of Canaan that got her daughter healed.

> *" 22 And behold, a woman of Canaan came from that region and cried out to Him, saying, "Have mercy on me, O Lord, Son of David! My daughter is severely demon-possessed."*
>
> *23 But He answered her not a word.*

And His disciples came and urged Him, saying, "Send her away, for she cries out after us."

[24] But He answered and said, "I was not sent except to the lost sheep of the house of Israel."

[25] Then she came and worshiped Him, saying, "Lord, help me!"

[26] But He answered and said, "It is not good to take the children's bread and throw it to the little dogs."

[27] And she said, "Yes, Lord, yet even the little dogs eat the crumbs which fall from their masters' table."

*[28] Then Jesus answered and said to her, "O woman, great is your faith! Let it be to you as you desire." And her daughter was healed from that very hour." (**Matthew 15:22-28**)*

Jesus again let the death arose because of the mercy he had on the plead from the widow.

"And it came to pass the day after, that he went into a city called Nain; and many of his disciples went with him, and much people.

Now when he came nigh to the gate of the city, behold, there was a dead man carried out, the only son of his mother, and she was a widow: and much people of the city was with her. And when the Lord saw her, he had compassion (mercy)on her, and said unto her, Weep not [11] *Now it happened, the day after, that He went into a city called Nain; and many of His disciples went with Him, and a large crowd.* [12] *And when He came near the gate of the city, behold, a dead man was being carried out, the only son of his mother; and she was a widow. And a large crowd from the city was with her.* [13] *When the Lord saw her, He had compassion on her and said to her, "Do not weep."* [14] *Then He came and touched the open coffin, and those who carried him stood still. And*

He said, "Young man, I say to you, arise." 15 So he who was dead sat up and began to speak. And He presented him to his mother..." **(Luke 7:11-15).**

None of those who sought the Lord's mercy left empty.

Mercy may be more specifically understood according to different categories, depending upon the areas where sin has had its effect; it also arouses the use of a variety of superlatives employed by the objects of such compassionate relief. Arthur Walkington for instance, suggests there are three aspects of God's mercy as follows:

- General mercy, to all of His creation. *"The LORD is good to all, and His mercies are over all His works"* (Psalm 145:9)

- Special mercy, to all of human-kind. *"Be sons of your Father who is in heaven; for He causes His sun to rise*

on the evil and the good, and sends rain
on the righteous and the unrighteous"
(Matthew 5:45).

- Sovereign mercy, to all heirs of
  salvation. *"For He says to Moses, 'I
  will have mercy on whom I have mercy,
  and I will have compassion on whom
  I have compassion. So then it does not
  depend on the man who wills or the man
  who runs, but on God who has mercy"*
  (Romans 9:15-16)

There are also distinctive qualities of
God's mercy:

- Great mercy. *"And Solomon said:
  "You have shown great mercy to Your
  servant David my father, because
  he walked before You in truth, in
  righteousness, and in uprightness of
  heart with You; You have continued this
  great kindness for him, and You have
  given him a son to sit on his throne, as it
  is this day '"* (I Kings 3:6).

- Covenant mercy. *"[5] And I said:*

"I pray, Lord God of heaven, O great and awesome God, You who keep Your covenant and mercy with those who love You[a] and observe Your[b] commandments," (Nehemiah 1:5).

- Abundant mercy. *"For You, Lord, are good, and ready to forgive, And abundant in mercy to all those who call upon You"* (Psalm 86:5).

- Everlasting mercy. *"But the mercy of the Lord is from everlasting to everlasting On those who fear Him, And His righteousness to children's children,"* (Psalm 103:17).

- Tender mercy. *"Through the tender mercy of our God, With which the Dayspring from on high has visited us;"* (Luke 1:78).

- Rich mercy. *"⁴ But God, who is rich in mercy, because of His great love with which He loved us,"* (Eph. 2:4).

- Full mercy. *"Indeed we count them blessed who endure. You have heard of the perseverance of Job and seen the end intended by the Lord – that the Lord is very compassionate and merciful"* (James. 5:11)

In the New American Standard translation, the word mercy is replaced by the expression, loving-kindness or by the term graciousness. These words convey a broader meaning than the word mercy as defined within the context of our discussion as compassion. Words over time take on slightly different meanings dictated by the contexts in which they are used. This is markedly noticeable in the King James translation of the Bible where old English definitions are used. In Scripture, there are two words that are almost inseparable: **forgiveness** and **mercy**. These are encapsulated in the word love. Jesus said:

" For God so loved the world that He gave His only begotten Son, that whoever

believes in Him should not perish but have everlasting life" (John 3:16).

It was God's great mercy that led Him to give His only begotten son as a ransom for first ancestor Adam, so that God could forgive Adam's transgression and recover the entire race from the eternal condemnation of sin and death. Jesus expressed the principle of forgiveness when he taught Peter to forgive seventy times seven.

"Jesus said to him, "I do not say to you, up to seven times, but up to seventy times seven." (Matthew 18:22).

And this was Jesus, the son of God and God incarnate who in Himself showed us what God looked like in character and nature. Therefore His command of we forgiving seventy times seven is a clue to the great forgiving heart of God.

David wrote: *"Have mercy upon me, O God, According to Your lovingkindness; According to the multitude of Your tender mercies, Blot out my transgressions"* (Psalm 51:1). God has promised that, through his great mercy, he would answer David's request and blot out the transgressions, not just of David, but of Israel and every member of the human race, giving each a chance to be restored back to divine favour.

God's Mercy is promised to all who are suffering and want to seek refuge. The bible makes us to understand that as the day approaches when all evil will be eradicated from the earth, and the Lord Almighty will stand up for His people, we will see these words fulfilled:

> *"But You, O Lord, shall endure forever, And the remembrance of Your name to all generations. You will arise and have mercy on Zion; For the time to favour her, Yes, the set time, has come."*

(Psalm 102:12, 13).

Here, we see the long-suffering God has had for Israel.

Today we see all kinds of calamities and sufferings plaguing man. We constantly hear, "Why does God permit all this suffering and pain?" Yet even in this, we see the mercy of our heavenly Father exhibited. The suffering of the people of Haiti from earthquake in 2010 and the devastation caused by earthquakes and other natural disasters around the world has been heart breaking to hear and watch. Still, as the Psalmist said, *"Weeping may last for the night, but a shout of joy comes in the morning"* (Psalm 30:5). God, in His wisdom, has used these tragedies to bring people together to teach them to be ready for "morning" when shouts of joy will ring in the air. The apostle John wrote that even tragedies like this will be handled by God's mercy in Christ's kingdom:

"He will wipe away every tear from their eyes; and there will no longer be any death; there will no longer be any mourning, or crying, or pain; the first things have passed away" **(Revelation 21:4).**

His mercy is the manifestation of His love. It is mirrored by compassion (affording help) in that it affords kindness in excess of what is expected or deserved.

"So none of the accursed things shall remain in your hand, that the Lord may turn from the fierceness of His anger and show you mercy, have compassion on you and multiply you, just as He swore to your fathers," **(Deuteronomy 13:17).**

It also carries the disposition of forgiveness.

Other expressions of mercy throughout scripture

The mercy of God can be described as God's response to the aide of His weak children. Our misery is sin, and because man is a sinner, he is considered miserable. But there is a very important distinction between misery and the one who is miserable and that is why God hates sin but loves the sinner; He loves the man who is weak and miserable. This love with which God loves man is defined as Mercy.

In the book of Jeremiah, the Lord Himself directed Himself to Israel and told them, "Return, rebel Israel...I will not remain angry with you; for I am merciful...I will not continue my wrath forever. Only know your guilt: how you rebelled against the Lord, your God" (Jeremiah 3:12-13). God tells us that He is kind to His people. He is kind and forgives the sins of His children who have repented of the evil they have done.

There are constant references in the Psalms to the mercy of God; however, the Prophet Jonah summarises very well what it means, for after having been angered, God forgave the people of Nineveh because they believed in Him and were converted. Jonah said,

> "So he prayed to the Lord, and said, "Ah, Lord, was not this what I said when I was still in my country? Therefore I fled previously to Tarshish; for I know that You are a gracious and merciful God, slow to anger and abundant in lovingkindness, One who relents from doing harm" **(Jonah 4:2).**

The entire book of the Prophet Jonah prepares us for the "evangelical revelation of the God of love" which is the greatest act of mercy that God has done for mankind: *"the Word became flesh and dwelt among us"* (Jonah 1:14). The Word became flesh so that we would come to know the love of God: "In this way the love of God was revealed to us: God sent his only Son into the world so that we might have life through him. In this is love: not that we have loved God, but that he loved us and sent his Son as expiation for our sins" *(1 John 4: 9-10).*

In order to save us, to free us from the evil one, sin, the world and the flesh, the Father sent His Son, so that through His words, works, passion, death and resurrection, He would redeem us, purchasing us with His blood and bringing us back into the Kingdom of God.

> *"For Christ, while we were still helpless, yet died at the appointed time for the ungodly… God proves his love for us in that while we were still sinners Christ died for us"* *(Roman 5:6, 8).*

This mercy continues to pour forth through the Church – especially in Confession and obedience to his Word. He came to nullify evil with good, to transform our sin into grace, and to transform our suffering into a means of sanctification. He went through the world "doing good."

The mercy pool is the basis for our continued blessing in the Lord. No wonder believers are called "vessels of mercy". "And He did so in order that He might make known the riches of His glory upon vessels of mercy, which He prepared beforehand for glory" *(Romans 9:23).*

God's past merciful dealings with us is the basis for our present encouragement. Those who walk according to the right kind of teaching come under a promise of His mercy.

> *"And as many as walk according to this rule, peace and mercy be upon them, and upon the Israel of God."* *(Galatians 6:16)*

We are therefore to continually pray that we may receive mercy in a time of our situations because mercy is a virtue that we are to exhibit towards others since special consideration will be shown at the Bema Seat to believers who show mercy to their neighbours. *" Blessed are the merciful, For they shall obtain mercy."* (Matthew 5:7)

Even though God's mercy endures forever, there is no mercy for unbelievers after death. It is therefore prudent for all to seek the mercies of God while on earth because after death God shall judge without mercy. Jesus Christ gave us an example of a rich man desiring mercy of forgiveness at the judgment day, but was not granted that mercy. Why not? Because he did not see the need in his lifetime to repent and obey God's commandments as given to Moses. Christ told this rich man, who desired mercy to be shown to his brothers, that what his brothers needed to do was to obey the law of Moses to receive mercy.

"And he cried and said, Father Abraham,

have mercy on me, and send Lazarus, that he may dip the tip of his finger in water, and cool my tongue; for I am tormented in this flame But Abraham said, Son, remember that thou in thy lifetime received thy good things, and likewise Lazarus evil things: but now he is comforted, and thou art tormented..." **(Luke16:24-31)**

"Then I saw a great white throne and Him who sat on it, from whose face the earth and the heaven fled away. And there was found no place for them. [12] And I saw the dead, small and great, standing before God,[a] and books were opened. And another book was opened, which is the Book of Life. And the dead were judged according to their works, by the things which were written in the books. [13] The sea gave up the dead who were in it, and Death and Hades delivered up the dead who were in them. And they were judged, each one according to his works. [14] Then

Death and Hades were cast into the lake of fire. This is the second death. [15] *And anyone not found written in the Book of Life was cast into the lake of fire."*
(Revelation 20:11-15)

No mercy will be shown towards judging the works of believers at the Judgment seat (Bema). God shows no mercy in judgment in time against those who persist in their rejection of His will. God's mercy does not negate His justice on the day of judgement. Let us not think we can trifle with His mercy and avoid any justice He must administer because of His holiness. Right now there is mercy that can be had in His greatest work of mercy, adoption into His family by and through His Son Jesus, but one day His mercy will step aside for justice.

Because of God's great mercies, we should rebound and present ourselves to God's service now without hesitation.

"I urge you therefore, brothers, by the mercies of God, to present your bodies a living and holy sacrifice, acceptable to God, which is your spiritual service of worship." **(Romans 12:1)**

In fact, when you go into the book of the Revelation - and indeed throughout the Bible - God is pictured and represented as being a great King, sitting on a throne with a rainbow about His throne. The rainbow is a representation of the mercy of God.

"Now Naaman, captain of the host of the king of Syria, was a great man with his master, and honourable, because by him the LORD had given deliverance unto Syria: he was also a mighty man in valour, but he was a leper..."
(2 Kings 5:1-27)

The story of Naaman shows us that God gives us victory over sicknesses, enemies and problems out of mercy even when we have not even known Him. Naaman was a man of valour but a leper yet he won battles against his enemies and he was healed by the mercy of God. There were times we came across death situations but miraculously, He rescued us even though at the end, we gave the glory to ourselves or somebody else.

The simple thing we must know is that God is a God of mercy. When He appeared to Moses, he declared his name before himself in these words: "...*The LORD, the LORD God, merciful and gracious, longsuffering, and abounding in goodness and truth....* " (Exodus 34:6). We see that in mercy he led his people forth out of Egypt to their habitation. Perhaps, one of the most repeated themes of praise in the Bible are the words, "His mercy endures forever." In Psalm 136 alone, this refrain is repeated 26 times.

It is God's mercy to which we sinners primarily appeal. We see this demonstrated in the words of the penitent David in Psalm 51:1: *"Have mercy on me, O God, according to your unfailing love; according to your great compassion blot out my transgressions."* The Father assures us in Psalm 147:11 that he is pleased with such an approach, for the Lord takes pleasure in those who fear him, in those who hope in his mercy. The devil always makes sinners to wrongly believe that God will justly deal with them and there is no mercy for them. But Jesus said He came for the lost. It is the wish that all might come to Him so that they may receive mercy. The mercy of God is in abundance now and it will be no more after death so seek him first while on earth and he shall grant you mercy over your life, your family and business.

"Blessed are the merciful: for they shall obtain mercy." **(Matthew 5:7)**

Chapter Five

MERCY AS A NEW BEGINNING

The power of mercy is most clearly demonstrated in the sacrificial death of Jesus on the cross since it was there that He overcame the power of justice by means of power of His compassion for the sinner. As a clarification of the above statement, we have to understand that justice is receiving what you deserve from the law but mercy sets judgement aside and gives clemency. It was at the cross that steadfast love and truth met; righteousness and peace have come together (Psalm 85:10), though it must be stressed that His reconciliation came at an enormous price to God Himself. It took the unimaginable strength for Jesus to willingly offer up Himself on the mercy seat in heaven. What we saw in Jesus on earth regarding his suffering and death was only a re-enactment of what He has actually done before we witnessed it. The scriptures refer to Him as the Lamb of God who was slain before the foundations of the world.

When we as believers see ourselves as we really are, when we have mourned over our condition, when we have walked in meekness before God and have yearned for righteousness, then it will attract mercy. The result is that not only do we embrace mercy for our benefit but we extend mercy to others as well. And it is because we recognise how much mercy has been extended to us. At that point we are now expected to recognise what the mercy of God can really do practically in our everyday lives.

The implication of the definitions of mercy as earlier discussed is in two fold. We would explore the first and deal with the second in the next chapter. The word *Mercy Seat* with reference to the Mercy Seat of the Ark of the Covenant was a symbol of the institutionalisation of mercy in the worship of Jehovah and His relationship with His people.

Mercy – To wipe Out Completely

The first of the meaning and the function of the mercy seat upon which mercy was obtained through the sprinkling of the blood, was *To wipe out completely.*

The words mercy seat has two meanings, *Kapporet* meaning to wipe out completely. It is the understanding of the priest and the people at the time that anytime the blood touched the mercy seat, the sins of the people have been completely atoned for. The sins, the misdemeanours, and the product of the human's sinful nature has been completely wiped out, giving them the opportunity to present themselves in God's presence as a holy people to merit the goodness and favour of God. The essence of the sprinkling of the blood was that, God is an absolute holy God and do not countenance anything unholy.

Therefore the person that comes to Him must be holy. This kind of holiness required was not attainable by works but through the shedding of blood, and therefore required the blood of animal for this cleansing process. However we are also told that the blood of these animals was also insufficient since it is humans that sin, they need the blood of humans to complete these cleansing process to enable humans to access the presence of God and have any form of fellowship with God. Therefore to release us from the burden of this cumbersome process, He sent His son to come in the form of a human and to die on behalf of all men. The consequence of this act on the behalf of men is that those who believe in Christ Jesus, are accepted on the basis of the sacrifice of Christ and don't have to die to pay for their sins or offer the blood of animals which is insufficient. It is the acceptance and application of the blood as though it is our own for the payment of the debt of our sins that mercy operates. Now let us look at a simple way to explain mercy from the *kapporet* as it relates to the *Mercy Seat,* **meaning to wipe out.**

The most simplest explanation by its extended meaning would be like a parent who gives his little child a slate to write on and later the child comes back to tell the parent that there is no space on the slate for her to write further again. The parent needs to clean over the slate to give the child a fresh space for her to write. The same happened when the blind man said

"Jesus son of David have mercy on me", what he really wanted Jesus to do for him was to wipe away his past and give him a new start or beginning. He was speaking from a perspective of having his past been wipe out and giving him a new beginning. There was no record that he was born blind or having been blind sometime after birth but all that he was asking Jesus was that he needed a new beginning. The same applies to most people today that need a new or a fresh start. Their past or present condition needs to be wiped out for a new beginning.

The dawn of a beginning has come for you through the blood to have a new beginning. It is about time, you tell yourself 'enough is enough'; you need a new opportunity to posses your possessions. May be most of your peers have gone far ahead of you in life because of your "blindness" but the time has come for you to receive your portion from the blood that was poured at the mercy seat. Jesus the son of David will show you mercy if you indeed called upon him.

Sometimes, some people think that if they get one thing that they need in life all their problems will be solved, such is not always true. The blind man never asked for only his eyes to get opened but he asked for mercy that means he wanted a new beginning of his life. Jesus might heal him all right but he might still not be able to enjoy life as he might wish, because he's had some of his productive years wasted. He wanted aside seeing, to have the mercy of God to have the opportunity to be fulfilled in life. That is why he asked for the mercy of God. He wanted a new opportunity to re-start his life. He was desperate to be breakout of his situation that has held him bound, restricted and limited for so long.

We have a similar incident occurring at the gate beautiful with Peter and John.

"Now Peter and John went up together to the temple at the hour of prayer, the ninth hour. [2] And a certain man lame from his mother's womb was carried, whom they laid daily at the gate of the temple which is called Beautiful, to ask alms from those who entered the temple; [3] who, seeing Peter and John about to go into the temple, asked for alms. [4] And fixing his eyes on him, with John, Peter said, "Look at us." [5] So he gave them his attention, expecting to receive something from them. [6] Then Peter said, "Silver and gold I do not have, but what I do have I give you: In the name of Jesus Christ of Nazareth, rise up and walk." [7] And he took him by the right hand and lifted him up, and immediately his feet and ankle bones received strength. [8] So he, leaping up, stood and walked and entered the temple with them — walking, leaping, and praising God. [9] And all the people saw him walking and praising God."
(Acts 3:1-9)

In the above passage, when the lame man asked Peter and John for alms, they understood what indeed the man needed which is not the alms he has been collecting from people who go to the temple to pray. The man needed a fresh beginning. One of the things that people do is that they deal with their challenges, which are likely to come back to them again. What people need to deal with are the limitations that create the challenges. The man was having a challenge of how to move about and getting alms from people. He might be probably satisfied with his life challenges because through the alms, he can send other people to get him what he needed at that moment.

But Peter and John saw that soliciting alms was just to deal with the challenge and will never solve his limitation in life. If he could walk, he could be working to fend for himself. Some of the things some people ask from God are not actually what they need. Some limitations need to be broken in order to deal with some of the challenges. If the limitations are dealt with, the challenges will be no more. The blind man understood this principle that is why he asked Jesus to wipe out his limitation so as to put him in the same level with his peers.

What some people ask from God are just to deal with the challenges but not the limitations that is why people always move from one challenge to the other because they have not been able to deal with the limitations of their lives. The blind man in the Luke account wanted a reverse of his situation so that he would make it in life. What you need is a fresh start and a new beginning.

Chapter Six

MERCY AS A JUDICIAL REVIEW OF LIFE CIRCUMSTANCES

Mercy - To rectify illegalities

The second meaning of the word *Kapporet* or mercy seat as it relates to the relationship that God has with His people, is to rectify illegalities. This is like how cases are determined at the law court. Usually, the Judge hears the case of both the plaintiff and the defendant and juxtapose them with the evidence available before determining whether or not the case has merit or otherwise. It is based on the evidence or the information given that the judge makes a pronouncement or judgment. If a court makes judgment based on evidence presented before the court and later found to have an error in examining evidence, forgery, or insufficient evidence or even in some cases new evidence emerges, a judge could order for a retrial which could result in the old conviction quashed.

This is a normal procedure in determining a case. If this occurs, there is a need for a judicial review or *Certiorari* by another court or judge on whether the previous judgment should stand or be quashed. When there is error in that process, it needs to be rectified. There is always a process that gives rise to that judgment and conviction in the first place, and has to be rectified through a judicial review at some point.

When the blind man said "Jesus son of David have mercy on me", all that he was saying was that there were some illegalities in his life that needed to be rectified. In the biblical context, something that is illegal is that which God has not ordained or sanctioned in one's life. Examples of illegalities in the life of an individual may include sickness, poverty, pain, failure, frustrations and all other life-boggling circumstances that have not been ordained or sanctioned by God.

They are therefore illegalities and need to be quashed by the blood of Jesus. The blind man got to know that his condition was not the purpose or the plan of God. Somehow he had this condition, which he never negotiated for or even deserved which he didn't like. His condition was an illegality, which for him had to be rectified for him to have a better and a new beginning. In the story of the man at the *Gate Beautiful*, John and Peter also saw an illegality in his condition, which by the power of God they rectified. It is time for you to rise and make sure this illegality is rectified.

The book of Ecclesiastes says that there has been wrong judgment against the people of God. Those who are to see the goodness of God are those who are suffering or have become servants. This is because they have not seen the power in the blood of Jesus that was sacrifice at the Mercy seat. People must claim what belongs to them from the hand of the wicked one.

> *"There is an evil I have seen under the sun,*
> *As an error proceeding from the ruler:*
> *⁶ Folly is set in great dignity, While*
> *the rich sit in a lowly place. ⁷ I have*
> *seen servants on horses, While princes*
> *walk on the ground like servants."*
> **(Ecclesiastes 10:5-7)**

The scripture above defines the form of illegality in another dimension basically stating that any lifestyle, condition, circumstance and state any person is in, that does not glorify God, demeans the person, condemns them to a life of destitution, dehumanises them and undermines their potential and worth is an illegality. Most of the time, the devil brings limitations in people's life in order to prevent them from getting what they really deserve in life. It may be barrenness, diseases, failings and other things of such sort.

Sometimes, the devil knows that if a child of God get what they desire from God or get some particular things in life, it will increase their faith and the devil cannot any longer operate in that area and sometimes in other areas of the person's life because he or she has been empowered through his or her faith to overcome him. The situation is that anytime God honours His word in the lives of His people, the devil is exposed as a liar and weakling in comparison to the might and power of God. It is about time that people of God realized that things must change in their lives. This illegality must stop; new opportunity must begin. People must go before God with faith based on His word and all the illegalities in their lives will be rectified.

There was this story about a man who went to a palm reader to seek how the future holds for him. The palm reader held the man's hands and told him all the challenges and crises he has gone through in life. The man listen to the palm reader so dejected because what the palm reader was telling him were true. The man then asked the palm reader what then does the future hold for me. The palm reader said by the time you get to the future, you are used to your past, which sadly is also your present condition. What the palm reader wanted the man to understand was that he has never acted on his bad situation in order to rectify it. The reason why he has not acted on the situation and wont act is because he is not desperate for a change in his circumstances. It is an error for children of God to be in some conditions, which make them unable to do what God expects them to do and yet don't have a strong urge to change that situation. Until people are desperate for a change in any situation they most of the time don't act, and without action there is no results. They always accept them as part of life. What children of God need to know is that until they get to a point where they want to wipe out their undesirable conditions and rectify things, things will never change for them.

Some may use flimsy excuses like 'with time, things will change'. Change will never come until you act. Time is neutral and takes on the properties that are applied to it. Someone has to apply some desirable life changing action to time for a desirable result. It is what you demand at that time that will bring change. Never compare yourself with other people who might be in similar situation. This is because you do not know what they did or what they are doing to get out of their situation. You must know that there is power in mercy seat of God as Christ sacrificed his blood so never accept your situation as it is. It is an error and an illegality for a child of God to experience the opposites of His Word in their lives.

Counterfeiting Mercy Through Available Substitutes

The power of God's mercy eradicates the legal hold of demonic powers (Mark 5:1-20). When we seek to have our legitimate needs fulfilled in an illegitimate way, we give room for spiritual influences of deception and death. Those influences take on the form of a false salvation, a false comfort, and false identity. The thing about deception is that it is so deceiving. No one ever seeks to be deceived. Every person seeks to fulfil the needs of their lives, but sometimes those needs get fulfilled in an illegitimate way. When this happens we become bound by a deceiving influence. It even sets up a force in our hearts that keeps our minds bound and our futures become limited. We become stuck and have no control in finding freedom. The power of God's mercy is enough to free us from the strongholds of deception. Demonic influences are no match to the mercy of God.

The power of God's mercy destroys the legal grounds by which a deceiving spirit abides. When the foundation of legal reasons for the lodging of deceptions is destroyed, there can no longer be a hold for demonic habitation. The power of God's mercy triumphs over every judgment. God's mercy makes way for the grace of God to fulfil the legitimate needs of our hearts in a life-giving way. Grace is the empowerment, but mercy is needed to reveal the true justification. That justification is the Father's love. It is God's mercy gave gave sight to the blind (Mark 10:47-52), and this same mercy will meet us in our blind conditions and justifies us to see. God's mercy is ever ready to empower your continued vision and give you the right to see. This can be physical, emotional, or spiritual. The condition of blindness calls out for the mercy of God! Mercy is a judgment and it eradicates every judgment of death. Sight comes because the power of God's mercy justifies us to see.

It is the power of God's mercy that causes us to be born again (1Peter 1:3). The power of God's mercy gives us a new beginning and releases us from the clutches of the hands of death and all other afflictions of life. True mercy was given by shed blood of Jesus Christ (Isaiah 53:5). It destroys every stronghold of the flesh and removes all judgments according to the flesh. We cannot expect to grow in God's grace without first be plugged out from our past through the power of His mercy. God invites us all to come to His throne of grace so we can first receive mercy and then be empowered by His grace. God's mercy transforms our "plea" to a justified "thank you". God's grace is empowered by our "thank you" and transforms us to the glory of God.

Chapter Seven

JESUS THE EMBODIMENT OF MERCY

For us to get a clearer understanding of the workings of mercy in our daily lives, believers need to know the relationship between the old tabernacle mercy seat and Christ in the New Testament.

Jesus, the light of the world

In the tabernacle and on the sanctuary, light came from the candelabra, representing Christ as the Light of the World, as well as the light of God's truth spread from activity of the seven churches.

Jesus said:

> *"Then Jesus spoke to them again, saying, "I am the light of the world. He who follows Me shall not walk in darkness, but have the light of life." (John 8:12) "I have come as a light into the world, that whoever believes in Me should not abide in darkness"* **(John 12:46)**

Jesus represents by the main branch of the lamp stand (candelabra), and the six branches that extend from original branch represent us as believers. Having believed, we are now living as "children of light" (Ephesians 5:8) who draw our source of light from Jesus, the true light. Jesus calls us "light of the world" and commands us to "let your light shine before men, that they may see your good deeds and praise your Father in heaven" **(Matthew 5: 14, 16)**. Not only so, but the branches serve as a picture of Jesus' description of our relationship with him: *"I am the vine, you are the branches … apart from me you can do nothing"* (John 15:5).

God is Light — the source of all light. People are in spiritual darkness until they receive revelation of the light of God. That is why Jesus became the Light of the world; He came to give us God's light — to reveal to us God's love and His will for us. John writes of Jesus, "In him was life, and that life was the light of men" (1:4). D. L. Moody, an American evangelist, reportedly told of a Christian woman who had been sick for months and was unable to leave her bed. But this woman was always cheerful. Someone asked her how she could be so happy when she could not even get outside to see the sun. She said, "My room is dark but I have the Son in my heart." Jesus was her inner source of spiritual light that drove away the gloom. He flooded her soul with His light and presence.

Jesus, the bread of life

On the table inside the tabernacle was a "Showbread" also called "bread of the presence" because it was to be always in the Lord's presence. The table and the bread were a picture of God's willingness to fellowship and communion (literally speaking, sharing something in common) with man. It was like an invitation to share a meal, an extension of friendship. Eating together often is an act of fellowship. God was willing for man to enter into His presence to fellowship with Him, and this invitation was always open.

Jesus exemplified this when He ate with tax collectors, prostitutes and the sinners of Jewish society. But this was more than just a gesture of friendship on earth. Jesus came to call sinners to Him, make them right with God, so that they could enjoy everlasting fellowship with God. Jesus had the Mercy for all, he wish that through him all will come in to know His father. He showed that He was, and He is the author of mercy. And this is encapsulated in the scripture from John 6.

"And Jesus said to them, "I am the bread of life. He who comes to Me shall never hunger, and he who believes in Me shall never thirst... This is the bread which comes down from heaven, that one may eat of it and not die" **(John 6:35, 49-50)**

God so desires our fellowship that He was willing to come to earth from heaven as our "bread of life" to give eternal life to all those who would partake in it. At Jesus' last Passover meal with His disciples, Jesus described Himself as bread again:

"While they were eating, Jesus took bread, gave thanks and broke it, and gave it to his disciples, saying, 'Take and eat; this is my body.'" **(Matthew 26:26)**

Jesus' broken body is our only access to fellowship with God. Today, we celebrate the Lord's Supper, or communion, to remember this important truth. And today, as in the day of Moses' tabernacle, God still desires to have fellowship and sit down for a feast with His people.

> " Behold, I stand at the door and knock. If anyone hears My voice and opens the door, I will come in to him and dine with him, and he with Me."
> **(Revelations 3:20)**

Christ was indeed the Bread of Life. Directly in front of one who entered the Holy Place, past the table of shewbread, stood the altar of incense, representing the prayers of the saints. Barring one's way into the Holy of Holies, into the very presence of God, was the veil. Once behind it, a person would be before the Mercy Seat, in the very presence of God. The veil being torn apart at Christ's death symbolises that a personal relationship with God can be established. The way had been opened by the sacrificial death of our Saviour. This intimate relationship with God is the key to our being transformed from glory to glory (2 Corinthians 3:18). If we cannot enter God's presence, if we are far away, there is not much hope of transformation. This is why the Bible so frequently urges us to seek God. Seeking God is part of "dressing and keeping" the relationship, helping it to grow. This close relationship is vital to increasing the Holy Spirit in us. He is the Lord of Mercy. Blessed are the merciful for they shall obtain mercy.

Jesus, our intercessor and the high priest

In the tabernacle was also the golden altar of incense representing the coming Christ, who is our intercessor before God the Father. During His days on earth, Jesus prayed for the believers. He was like the high priest of the tabernacle, who bore the names of each of the Israelite tribes on his breastplate before God.

The office of priest was an important one in the Old Testament system and Jesus fulfilled it. In the Jewish system, a priest mediated between the people and God. Aaron and his descendants were appointed priests, with the tribe of Levi serving as assistants in the Tabernacle (Numbers 3:5-10). The Levites were viewed as belonging to God (Numbers 3:12); they were set apart. The high priest was the chief religious leader and had certain duties.

Among those duties were wearing the Urim and Thummin to assist in determining the will of God and overseeing the other priests. Most importantly, it was the high priest who entered into the Most Holy Place on the Day of Atonement. Only the high priest could enter and, before doing so, he was required to make a sacrifice for himself. In this way, the high priest was cleansed and could then go on to offer the cleansing sacrifices for the people (Leviticus 16).

Jesus as High Priest mediates for us. His sacrifice is what provides cleansing for our sins. Rather than a yearly (or daily) atonement, Jesus' sacrifice is once-for-all. Jesus like the high priests of Old Testament time stands in the gap between us (the people) and God. He made the necessary sacrifice for us (Jesus was without sin so did not need to offer a sacrifice for Himself as did the high priests of the Old Testament).

We have been made righteous by Jesus (2 Corinthians 5:21) and are now able to enter into God's presence. This mediation of Jesus is permanent and continual. Hebrews 7:23-25 says,

> *"The former priests were many in number, because they were prevented by death from continuing in office, but he holds his priesthood permanently, because he continues forever."*

While Jesus' sacrifice was once-for-all, His mediation for us continues. Jesus also communicates the will of God to us through His teachings and through the Holy Spirit (John 14:26). Jesus is not only our High Priest, but also a "priest forever after the order of Melchizedek" (Hebrews 7:11-22). Melchizedek is introduced in the bible as both a king and a priest (Genesis 14:18). He met Abram (later known as Abraham) after Abram's battle victory.

In their meeting, Melchizedek blessed Abram, and Abram gave him a tenth of everything, thus confirming Melchizedek's priesthood and authority. The writer of Hebrews explains that Jesus is of this order of priests – His priesthood is based on authority rather than on lineage (Hebrews 7:11-17), and it is also kingly. Therefore, Jesus' priesthood institutes a new way of being: *"For when there is a change in the priesthood, there is necessarily a change in the law as well"* (Hebrews 7:12). With Jesus as High Priest, a new covenant is in effect. Perhaps the most crucial thing for believers to understand today is that it is because Jesus is our High Priest that we can approach God with confidence (Hebrews 4:16). We no longer need to go through earthly mediators. Jesus has broken the barrier, made the sacrifice, established a new covenant, and reinstituted our relationship with God. Because of our High Priest, we are free to come to God.

Today, Jesus still is our high priest at the Father's side, interceding for God's people. Let me share a story I read from a friend of mine on his Facebook wall.

A lady committed a crime and she was sent to court. The punishment for the crime was life imprisonment. She shed tears for help but to no avail.

When the case was called in court, she started weeping. Her husband, family and friends who accompanied her started doing the same since there was no hope. But something happened. Before the lady could stand in the witness box, a man stood up and the court room was silent. Everyone looked at Him. He was noble and gentle.

He stood in the witness box and interceded on behalf of the woman. The case was difficult, yet He used all His strength, energy and resources to fight on behalf of the woman. After a long legal battle between the man and the accusers, the lady was set free. The lady fell before the man and asked 'WHO ARE YOU?'

The next day, the lady deliberately committed another crime and was sent to the same court. As soon as she entered the courtroom, she saw the man who interceded for her the previous day on the judgement seat.

He was no longer a lawyer, but a judge. With smiles on her face, the lady said 'I have come again' The man lifted his head and said 'yesterday I was a lawyer, so I fought for you, even when you were guilty. But today I am a judge and my judgement must be fair.' With tears in the ladies eyes she asked for the second time 'WHO ARE YOU' and the man replied 'I AM THE SAVIOUR'. Today Christ Jesus is our lawyer , redeemer and intercessor but a day is coming when He will give a fair judgement to everyone.

Today, through the blood of Christ, we can come boldly in prayer in Jesus' name. When we pray in Jesus' name, we are praying based on the work He has done and not on our own merit. It is in His powerful name that we are saved and baptised, and in His name we live, speak and act.

> *"And I will do whatever you ask in my name, so that the Son may bring glory to the Father. You may ask me for anything in my name, and I will do it."*
> **(John 14:13-14)**

"Christ Jesus, who died — more than that, who was raised to life — is at the right hand of God and is also interceding for us." **(Romans 8:34)**

" I am the good shepherd: the good shepherd giveth his life for the sheep 12 But he that is an hireling, and not the shepherd, whose own the sheep are not, seeth the wolf coming, and leaveth the sheep, and fleeth: and the wolf catcheth them, and scattereth the sheep.
13 The hireling fleeth, because he is an hireling, and careth not for the sheep. 14 I am the good shepherd, and know my sheep, and am known of mine. 15 As the Father knoweth me, even so know I the Father: and I lay down my life for the sheep. I am the good shepherd. The good shepherd gives His life for the sheep.[12] *But a hireling, he who is not the shepherd, one who does not own the sheep, sees the wolf coming and leaves the sheep and flees; and the wolf catches the*

sheep and scatters them. ¹³ The hireling flees because he is a hireling and does not care about the sheep. ¹⁴ I am the good shepherd; and I know My sheep,and am known by My own. ¹⁵ As the Father knows Me, even so I know the Father; and I lay down My life for the sheep."
(John 10:11-15)

Our Lord is, and always will be, the one Mediator between man and God. But let us acknowledge that whenever an unsaved sinner comes to God through God's chosen Mediator, Jesus fulfils the function of the Old Covenant *Mercy Seat* by becoming the genuine meeting place between God and the believing sinner. In other words, man and God really meet in Jesus Christ when saving faith occurs. Unlike the inanimate *Mercy Seat* of Moses' day, the risen and living Jesus Christ "introduces" the sinner to God. And He does so by bestowing eternal life—God's life—on the one who believes, so that the believer knows God. *"For there is one God, and one mediator between God and men, the man Christ Jesus"* **(John 17:3)**

"For there is one God, and one mediator between God and men, the man Christ Jesus" (Romans 8:33). Although the persons in the Godhead are equal in essence and glory, their differing roles must always be noted. Jesus in His role as Mediator bestows eternal life on the believer thus introducing Him to God. God in response accepts the believing sinner and pronounces him justified. The believer then meet God in the Person of God's living *Mercy Seat,* our Lord and Saviour Jesus Christ. God has behaved righteously and graciously in response to His Son. Thus He has been *"just and the justifier of the one who has faith in Jesus"*

> *"21 But now the righteousness of God without the law is manifested, being witnessed by the law and the prophets;*

²² Even the righteousness of God which is by faith of Jesus Christ unto all and upon all them that believe: for there is no difference

²³ For all have sinned, and come short of the glory of God;

²⁴ Being justified freely by his grace through the redemption that is in Christ Jesus:

²⁵ Whom God hath set forth to be a propitiation through faith in his blood, to declare his righteousness for the remission of sins that are past, through the forbearance of God;

²⁶ To declare, I say, at this time his righteousness: that he might be just, and the justifier of him which believeth in Jesus." **(Romans 3:21-26)**

EPILOGUE

A little boy came running into the house after playing outside. His mother stopped him and asked what was on his hand. He replied, "Oh, just a little mud." His mother then asked if he was planning on getting it off his hand. He thought for a moment and said, "Sure, Mom. I'll just wipe it off with my other hand." There was only one problem with the plan, one dirty hand plus one clean hand equals two dirty hands.

Many people are like that little boy; they see the evil and wrongs in their life and think they can make themselves clean by bringing the good in their life to bear on the problem. But it does not work that way.

We all need a way to be made morally and spiritually clean, and we will never succeed in doing it ourselves. The only solution is to be found in the blood of Jesus Christ, which cleanses us from all sins.

The message of mercy is that God loves us — all of us — no matter how great our sins have been and are. Devotion to the divine mercy involves a total commitment to God as Mercy. It is a decision to trust completely in Him, to accept His mercy with thanksgiving, and to be merciful as He is merciful. He wants us to recognise that His mercy is greater than our sins, so that we will call upon Him with trust, receive His mercy, and let it flow through us to others. Thus, all will come to share His joy. It is a message we can call to mind simply by remembering ABC.

A — Ask for His Mercy. God wants us to approach Him in prayer constantly, repenting of our sins and asking Him to pour His mercy out upon us and upon the whole world. Solomon wisely wrote about 3000 years ago, *"There is a time for everything."* (Ecclesiastes 3:1) And I would like to encourage you to realise that now is the time to ask for God's mercy. We are still living in a day where your request can receive mercy and forgiveness. The time is coming, however, when each one of us will come before the Judge. And on that day, those without a white robe will no longer have the opportunity to accept Jesus and receive mercy.

Jesus once shared a story with His disciples about two men who went to the temple for prayer. One was a publican, a civil worker, and one was a teacher or Rabbi. Both men had come to ask God for repentance of their sins. The Rabbi began his plea by thanking God that he was not like the publican who was standing close by. On the contrary, the publican entered the Temple and began his plea by beating his chest in a sign of surrender and humility. He then made this powerful statement in prayer: "God have mercy on me, a sinner". This publican, probably a foremost chief of sinners, first of all knew who he was; a sinner in need of repentance, and secondly a man in need of the mercy of the Lord. Like this Publican, we must recognise who we are, sinners in need of the mercy of the Lord. What is an absolute necessity for the people is the mercy of God.

B — Be merciful. God wants us to receive His mercy and let it flow through us to others. He wants us to extend love and forgiveness to others just as He does to us. Practice the "golden rule" of Jesus. Luke 6:27-31 "But I tell you who hear me: Love your enemies, do good to those who hate you, bless those who curse you, pray for those who mistreat you. If someone strikes you on one cheek, turn to him the other also. If someone takes your cloak, do not stop him from taking your tunic. Give to everyone who asks you, and if anyone takes what belongs to you, do not demand it back. Do to others as you would have them do to you"

C — Completely trust in Jesus. God wants us to know that the graces of His mercy are dependent upon our trust. The more we trust in Jesus, the more we will receive. As we trust the Lord in the midst of our darkness, troubles, sicknesses and in desperate moments, His mercy will come pursuing after us and be made manifest in ways unimaginable "above all that we could ask or even think". It was David who witnessed the truth of this when he found himself walking "in the valley of the shadow of death" (Psalm 23). There, in the darkness of the shadows, came goodness and mercy following after. The word "follow" in the Hebrew denotes the military term for pursuing an enemy or group that has taken off on the run either in retreat or for regrouping and is a command that the commanding officer would give to the troop(s). When we trust God, He orders the pursuit. When mercy caught up to David there was found prepared a table before him even in the presence of his enemies with an overflowing cup of the blessings of the Lord

Remember God's mercy only come through the sprinkling of Jesus' blood that happened when He died on Calvary. That blood is able to wipe your past clean and also to rectify every illegality in your life. The mercy of God would rewrite your life.

NOTES

Ron J. Bigalke, Jr. (2002). *Christ As The "Mercy Seat": Understanding The Shed Blood Of Christ*

Wehrfritz-Hanson, G. (2006). *Bartimaeus: From blind beggar to seeing disciple*
Retrieved from http://www.sermoncentral.com/sermons/bartimaeus-from-blind-beggar-to-seeing-disciple-garth-wehrfritz-hanson-sermon-on-gods-forgiveness-96799.asp?Page=3

Robredillo, L. C. (2012). *Blind Bartimaeus: A Disciple Who Recognizes and Follows Jesus with the Eyes of Faith*
Retrieved from http://www.cbcpnews.com/cbcpnews/?p=6704

GoodSeed International (2000). *The Tabernacle Place*
Retrieved from http://the-tabernacle place.com/articles/what_is_the_tabernacle/tabernacle_holy_of_holies

Pope, K. (2014). *Christ: Our Mercy Seat*. Accessed from http://ancientroadpublications.com/Studies/BiblicalStudies/MercySeat.html

Compelling Truth (2011). *How is Jesus our High Priest?* Accessed from http://www.compellingtruth.org/Jesus-high-priest.html

Hodges, Z. (2010). *Propitiation and the Holy of Holies* Retrieved from http://www.faithalone.org/magazine/y2006/06ja1.html

McLaughlin, R. R. (2009). *The Doctrine of Mercy* Retrieved from http://www.gbible.org/index.php?proc=tre&sf=rea&tid=497

Humphreys, K. *God's Mercy Toward Mankind* Retrieved from http://www.heraldmag.org/2011/11jf_5.htm

Phillips, G. *Mercy* Retrieved from https://www.raptureready.com/featured/phillips/phillips81.html

Goodwin, T. (2007). *The Works of Thomas Goodwin* Retrieved from http://webcache.googleusercontent.com/search?q=cache:9rjQceaw90AJ:www.bunyanministries.org/expositions/attributes/08_Mercy.pdf+&cd=11&hl=en&ct=clnk&gl=gh

Laurie G. *Mercy is an action?* Retrieved from
http://www.jesus.org/life-of-jesus/teaching-and-
messages/mercy-is-an-action.html

See article at http://pastorstrom.com/millennial/
teaching-of-gods-eternal-mercy/
Fr John H. Hapsch (2006). *The Awesome Mercy of
God*, Servant Books.
Unknown Author, https://www.historicengland.
org.uk/research/inclusive-heritage/disability-
history/1050-1485/

Melanie Close, Disability History in Britain,
Disbility Equality, 2011, 1.

BOOKS BY THE AUTHOR

THROUGH
The
EYES OF GOD

This is a book intended to provide alternative principles to the 'success motivation' principles that deal with the material aspect of man's existence without approaching the concept of success from a holistic perspective to include the spirit and the soul of the human, which in addition to the body (material aspect) form its constituents.

Life is a system that has constituent parts. The behaviour of a system depends on how every one of its inter-related constituents functions. Therefore, the outcome of a person's life rests on the inter-related function of the spirit, soul and body and the principles that are fed into them.

You will discover from his book a detailed examination of the principles, concepts and peculiarities of the kind of building God wants us to build.

BREAKING
The
SIEGE

There are many things that the Christian life can be likened to. These similes and metaphors grow out of the distinctive perspectives we hold of Christianity. These perspectives are developed as a result of our individual understanding of scripture, our personal experiences with God, and distinct encounters with both human and spirit entities in our universe.

One of the strategies the enemy uses against the church and members of the body of Christ is the siege, which most people know little about, or maybe entirely ignorant about.

Through this book, you will understand what a siege is all about, how you would know you are under siege and how to break any form of siege in your life.

THE GATES
THE
ENEMIES
AND YOU

The concepts of *'gates'* has been overlooked as part of the promised blessing of God upon Abraham, and has often been subjected to wrong interpretations. This has been the case because, the meaning and functions of the 'gates' as understood in biblical times has gone through changes in what it may mean in our world today.

Dr Appiah uses the rich interconnectedness of the interpretation, analysis and application of the scriptural text with the facts and information of history to bring home the understanding of the subject.

You will discover through this book:
• The constitution of the 'gates' as an entity and its functions.
• The keys with which you take full control of ones' enemy 'gates'.
• Certain mistakes of history the church universal and various local churches are repeating to diminish the prevailing authority of the church against the ' gates' of hell.
• How you can realise the Blessing of Abraham in its entirety in your life.

Available in print and electronic versions at
iTunes
Amazon
Barnes and Noble
Christianbooks.com
eden.co.uk
.. and other online book retailers and a bookshop near you

The POWER of MERCY

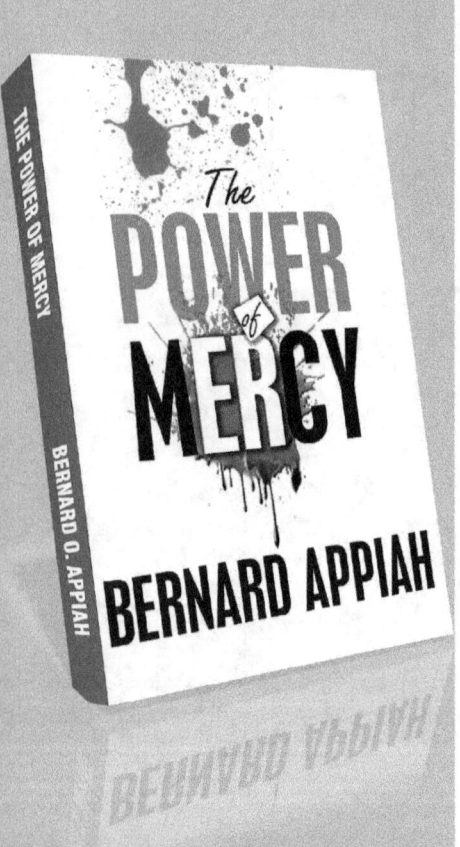

Today, mercy is one of the overused terms in contemporary evangelical Christianity. As a result, it has been passed around as a jargon without its latent power of transformation being examined closely in the light of the scriptures.

In this book Dr Bernard Appiah; turn to the scriptures to explore the subject of mercy. From the Old Testament, he delves into the institutionalisation of mercy in God's relationship with His people, by examining the significance of the Mercy Seat located on the Ark of the Covenant, which represented the government and presence of God among His people. In the New Testament, he examines the subject through the coming of Jesus Christ, His mission and His death by the shedding of His blood. From that, he explains the implication of the scriptural understanding of God's mercy for us today.

Dr Appiah uses a biblical narrative of Jesus' encounter with a blind 'non-believer' as a bridge to the Old Testament, to explore the idea of mercy from two distinct perspectives namely; to wipe out completely, and a call for a judicial review in the life of every individual who calls upon God for mercy.

ADDING VALUE *to* INCREASE *your* WORTH

We all have a basic intrinsic value determined by God at the time of creation and as a confirmation, Jesus stated that humans as the apex of God's creation has more value than animals and for that reason God even cares more about us.

From this point on, it is the responsibility for all humans to add to this basic intrinsic value conferred on us at the time of creation to increase our worth, which will enable us to stand out of the crowd. Ever heard of this statement, "It is crowded at the bottom"? It would therefore take adding value to yourself to stand out of the crowd.

On the basis of this, Dr Appiah draws principles from different disciplines of personal development, including management, biological science, religion (Christianity), psychology and others for increasing our worth through adding value to ourselves.